YOU CAN'T STOP THE
SUN FROM SHINING

YOU CAN'T STOP THE SUN FROM SHINING

SONNY BILL WILLIAMS

WITH ALAN DUFF

HODDER &
STOUGHTON

First published in Great Britain in 2021 by Hodder & Stoughton
An Hachette UK company

1

Copyright © Sonny Bill Williams 2021

Picture section design by Christabella Designs
All images courtesy of Sonny Bill Williams unless otherwise credited

A CIP catalogue record for this title is available from the British Library

Hardback ISBN 9781529387858
Trade Paperback ISBN 9781529397390
eBook ISBN 9781529387865

Printed and bound in Great Britain by Clays Ltd, Elcograf S.p.A.

Hodder & Stoughton policy is to use papers that are natural, renewable
and recyclable products and made from wood grown in sustainable forests.
The logging and manufacturing processes are expected to conform to the
environmental regulations of the country of origin.

Hodder & Stoughton Ltd
Carmelite House
50 Victoria Embankment
London EC4Y 0DZ

www.hodder.co.uk

This book is dedicated to my mum and dad

CONTENTS

Introduction
by Alan Duff

I might be the last person you'd expect to find working with Sonny Bill on his autobiography. I've written eleven novels, two adapted to feature films, and three non-fiction books, and I'm a former syndicated newspaper columnist, now writing for television. I'm not a professional sports writer.

But, like most Kiwis, I love rugby – even though I played my last game almost thirty-two years ago, and at a low level. My meagre claim to representative success is playing for the Canterbury under-15s a long, long time ago. I had a season of rugby league as a young man, so I know first-hand what a tough game it is. And I have loved boxing since I fell in love with Cassius Clay, who later changed his name to Muhammad Ali to reflect his new religion, Islam. Of course, sporting colossus Sonny Bill is also a Muslim convert, and more than a few pundits have compared the two athletes. This pundit happens to believe that they share more than just unique athletic ability; they are both known for being exceptionally decent human beings, doing good for the wider community. As Tom Humphries observed in the *Irish Times* in 2010:

> Every now and then a sport gets gifted a character who seems destined to transcend its boundaries and become something more broadly iconic. An Ali. A George Best. A Babe Ruth. A Joe Namath. Rugby has found one such. Sonny Bill Williams . . . Even to the untrained eye he is something special.

Like many, I was onto the phenomenon of Sonny Bill from the time of his incredible NRL debut for the Canterbury Bulldogs at the supposed-to-be-tender age of just eighteen. I say 'supposed to be' because he was as far from physically and mentally tender as it gets. Humphries described him as 'granite'.

I met Sonny Bill for the first time in Paris at the end of 2017, when he was touring with the All Blacks and I was preparing to return home to New Zealand after almost a decade of self-exile. He was accompanied by his inimitable manager, Khoder Nasser, and it was then that a collaboration between us was first discussed. Khoder suggested that being 'outsiders' gave the three of us a certain affinity. And so it has proved: we all feel we're a good match when it comes to getting Sonny's story on these pages.

Sonny Bill is considered a sports superstar throughout the rugby and league world. Throw in New Zealand heavyweight boxing champion and All Blacks Sevens Olympian and there you have it: a sporting hero like no other before him. But as Sonny Bill shared his life story with me, other qualities emerged. I learned of his humility and extreme modesty – indeed, shyness. I would discover a courage that went beyond that found on rugby fields and in the boxing ring. He is strong-minded, a man of unwavering principles. And EMPATHY has to be in capital letters because he has it by the bucketload.

Many of Sonny's personal qualities can be attributed to his religion. To become a Muslim – or start the process of conversion, at least – only a few years after 9/11, when most of the Western world considered Islam and terrorism to be inextricably linked, takes more than courage. That decision not only put his stellar sporting reputation at risk, it exposed him to the odium of the prejudiced and the ignorant, and not a few otherwise rational people whose minds had been turned by those horrific attacks. Sonny will tell you he was no different: he once conflated Islam with terrorism, as I did myself. But through its teachings, Sonny discovered a deep inner healing and peace. He is living proof that the basic tenets of Islam preach goodness, charity, humility and a love of Allah. No, he has not converted me, and he never attempted to, but he has taught me to be more open-minded.

With Sonny living in Sydney and me in Auckland, we were forced by Covid-19 to conduct our exchanges on Zoom, but we quickly warmed to each other. Sonny Bill would begin each two-hour session by asking: 'How are you, Alan? How's your family? You all good?' He is a listener, not someone who is tripping over himself to talk about Sonny Bill the big sports star. Far from it. The more we talked, the more I would gently push him to go deeper. Although Sonny is modest and without ego, he is not secretive, and he didn't shy away from discussing personal issues. This book is about getting to know the real Sonny Bill Williams, who at a young age went from obscurity to becoming the subject of headlines and media-hyped controversies.

Some of the negative media coverage of Sonny over the years really bothered me, and I'll admit I wanted payback, but Sonny is bigger than that. He has no interest in naming names or throwing anyone under the bus. And in any case, Sonny Bill's actions speak louder than their words. Watch a replay of what happened after the Rugby World Cup 2015, when young fan Charlie Line was tackled by a security officer as he ran onto the ground during the triumphant All Blacks team victory walk. Observe Sonny's body language, how he helps Charlie up and walks him back to his parents before taking off his gold medal and putting it around the kid's neck, hugging him. Instead of losing his head in all that joyful clamour around him, he put this young kid's welfare first. You are probably aware of that incident, but you're probably not aware that he stayed in contact with Charlie and his parents, just as you do not know of Sonny Bill's countless other acts of kindness and empathy.

That trait came through in every talk session we have had. 'Bro' and 'my bro' he uses frequently. It has got to the point where he's got this old codger saying the same, not just to him and Khoder, but to my mates as well! His desire to use his profile to help lift Pacific Islanders and Māori was declared from the start. To my mind, he grew another 6 feet 4, standing there like a rigid sentinel willing to die to protect/inspire his/our Polynesian people. He made sure the photographer who took the photo for the cover of this book was of Pasifika background, and ensured one of the editorial staff was too.

You hear that a few times and you start to realise that this project – being this guy – is bigger than this ardent admirer realised. Sonny Bill tells of being heavily influenced by Malcolm X. This reminded me that I read

Malcolm X's book years back and now at least can refer to YouTube video interviews with this extraordinary African American, a reformed ex-inmate from the ghetto who discovered Islam and dared to tell white America that their appalling abuse of black Americans made them no less than 'devils'. An accusation that obviously did not go down well with white America.

Sonny is not for one moment echoing those same thoughts. But an awful lot of what Malcolm X had to say on white racism rings bells with him, as they still do with me. Listening to Malcolm X talk brings on a series of 'hey, of course!' moments. Like I experienced decades ago while going through my Muhammad Ali adoration period, my astonishment at Malcolm X's utterances are echoed by Ali. But both men's legacies continue to echo down the ages and inspire younger men of colour to stand taller.

When you're a younger adult still forming your views on life, some incredible insights get slowly consumed by your own maturity. But those notions that are still sticking forty years later? Well, that's wisdom and righteousness resonating down the generations.

I have found in Sonny Bill a whole bunch of righteous notions, going from faint to thundering down the years as he became more self-aware thanks to his conversion to Islam. The man who wanted so much to become a better person is well on the way to achieving that.

He is determined to do what he can to help lift brown people – Polynesians, including we Māori who came from the Pacific islands around 1250. To be an example to youngsters so they might aim for his heights, in sports, in business, professional careers – anything but menial employment forever doomed to live on Struggle Street. And to remind them not to ignore their own moral compass as they find their way. His desire just to be a decent human being is the motivation behind much of what he does now.

He donated a large sum of money to the Christchurch earthquake fund because he was there, playing for the Canterbury Crusaders, when that shattering event occurred in 2011. He went back to Christchurch in 2019 to comfort his fellow Muslims after fifty-one people were slaughtered by a madman while praying in their mosques.

When I speak of Sonny Bill's greatness, I don't just mean it in terms of his sporting genius, in the sense of him being 'biggest', 'fastest', 'strongest' or 'cleverest'. I mean it in the sense of the largeness of his heart for the wider world.

Every writer working with sporting heroes will claim to be privileged and humbled by the opportunity. Well, I'm no different: I am both. But I'll go further than that and say that being involved in this story is a gift. The last thing Sonny wants is for me to sprinkle these pages with praise. 'Water off a duck's back, bro,' is how he handles the adulation. 'I just strive to be a better person. A better husband, father, friend, citizen.' He insists that he is ordinary, but Sonny Bill is far from that. He is truly extraordinary, not just as a sportsman but as a man, as this book will show.

And with that, I will hand you over to Sonny.

Alan Duff

2021

CHAPTER 1

Sleeping with my boots on

I was around seven years old, lying awake on a Friday night while my parents partied in the lounge room. But it wasn't their singing that was keeping me up; it was excitement – because Saturday was footy day. So even though I was in bed, I was fully dressed for the game in my club jersey, shorts, long socks . . . even my footy boots.

I thought about footy constantly. Thanks to my brother, Johnny, I already knew the names of some of the famous rugby league players in the NRL. Johnny, who is two years older, was a very good player. Our old man had been a top player too, but, as he said himself, he'd blown his chance to make the big time because he wasn't focused enough. He later coached age-group teams for years, and every one of his teams won their championship.

I lived for winter Saturdays and played footy at lunchtime and after school, while at home I passed, kicked, tackled and discussed the game endlessly with Johnny. I ignored bad weather; I just wanted to play. When there weren't enough numbers to make up teams, a few of us kids would still get together and practise. That's where my offloads were born.

My entire family was obsessed with the NRL, so it's no surprise I was too. Rugby league was always part of what we did and what we talked about. And it didn't just come from my old man's Sāmoan side of the family; my white half-Australian mum's family was into it too. Mum's father, William 'Bill' Woolsey, had been a top league player as well as a boxer and bar-room brawler. His reputation was fierce, on and off the field. So rugby league was in my genes, and I guess I was lucky enough to be born with sporting talent.

* * *

Fast-forward about eleven years to 2004 and a dream was on the verge of coming true. I was in Sydney, in the Canterbury Bulldogs changing room, about to make my NRL debut at age eighteen against the Parramatta Eels. And guess what? I'd forgotten my boots! I must have been that nervous packing my stuff. Seven-year-old me would have been shocked. At that moment, I wished I'd slept in them.

A team talk started but I couldn't concentrate properly; all I could think was, *What do I do, I don't have any boots?* I was panicking. Without a word to anyone, I slipped outside to look for my brother in the crowd. Johnny saw me and waved, and I ran over and told him the problem. I asked him if he could drive home fast and get my boots, but he said he didn't need to: he had a new pair in his car that I'd given him when they'd issued us players with heaps of free gear. Phew!

After that, I remember warming up. It was a surreal feeling, the same feeling I would experience some years later playing my first game for the All Blacks. Thinking, *Is this really happening?* But at least I knew the Bulldogs players; I'd been hanging around the club the last two years as a young guy on a league scholarship, and even the most feared senior players had been kind and encouraging. I'd practised with them and guys like giant Willie Mason and Matt Utai had inspired me. So many of them went out of their way to make me feel welcome and treat me like I was one of them, even before I took the field alongside them. But I still felt like an outsider and was aware I had a lot to prove.

Hearing the crowd coming into Telstra Stadium, I knew that this was it. All those years of watching NRL and playing with my mates back home, all the practising and training were about to pay off . . . I hoped. The noise and excitement of the fans emphasised the significance of the moment. In a few minutes, my career was about to start. It was really, really daunting.

There were others having their debut in that game too, like Willie Tonga, Reni Maitua and Hutch Maiava – and though future Hall of Famer Johnathan Thurston had made his debut two years earlier playing first grade for the Bulldogs, I know he was as nervous and fired up as I was that day. Us novices got on well, so we all looked out for each other, but really, with any debut, you are on your own. It is up to you to put in the effort and play a good game.

The whistle blew and it was on. Starting off with a big shoulder-charge hit put an end to my nerves. And before I knew it, the game was over! We'd won 48–14, and after the final whistle I heard my name being chanted by the crowd. How could that be?

Afterwards, the team went out drinking and celebrating. Many in that Bulldogs team trained hard, played hard and partied hard. I had proved I could match them on the field, but there was no way I could match them off it. At that point, I didn't even want to try. I didn't drink and I was still the shy new fella, not comfortable in a social setting with guys who seemed full of self-confidence and knew so much more than I did. If there were more than two people in a room, I struggled to speak up. So, after one of the biggest moments of my life to date, I went home to my old man's place with Johnny. Dad had moved to Australia by then. I can remember us in my old man's lounge room rewatching the game together. I was sitting there and I was spinning. I'd look at Johnny and it was like, *Bro, did that just happen? Did I really just play NRL?* And he'd look at me and he's asking the same thing. After the colour, noise and frenetic activity of the game, I was pinching myself. It all felt like a dream. My old man, being the typical Islander father that he was, kept standing up and walking around, laughing and saying out loud to no-one but us, 'That's my son. That's my son.'

I'd paid for Johnny to come over and join me in Sydney six months before that debut. Even though Dad was here, I was missing family and Johnny had been getting into some serious trouble back home, so it seemed like a great opportunity for a fresh start. I found a dope pipe in his trouser pocket not long after he arrived; that's the state he was in at the time. He knew he was on a bad path, and it was one he didn't want me to follow. Johnny had been adamant that I accept the offer to go to the Bulldogs in Sydney as a teenager because he didn't want me to end up like him, in trouble with the law, selling weed, drinking, fighting, running with the wrong crowd. I was a mama's boy and wanted to stay home, but Johnny said, 'Bro, you've got to go or you're going to end up where I am.'

John Arthur – Johnny – was a talented footballer but everyone thought of him as the 'bad' brother. He was never a bad brother to me. (As far as our mum was concerned, if she answered the phone and someone asked for either Johnny or Sonny, she'd say no-one of that name lives here. We have a John Senior, a John Arthur and a Sonny Bill.) I credit Johnny with so much of my success because he's always had my back. He'd practise with me, gee me up when my confidence was low – he made me want to do better on the field to impress him. Johnny would deal with bullies who hassled me. When he was around, I felt safe. I didn't have to be anyone but myself with him. When I played well, he felt as if he'd played well with me. If I struggled with a personal problem, he struggled with me. My big uso (brother) was always there for me, ready to listen and keep me company.

My old man – John Senior – was pretty hard on us growing up. It wasn't like he didn't praise us, but often a compliment came with a longer critical assessment of what we'd done as well. Sometimes that was difficult for my brother and me to cop. Nowadays, he is a very different man. He often tells me how proud he is of me and says, 'I love you, son.' But back then – like a lot of Kiwi rugby and rugby league dads, so it's not just a Sāmoan thing – his attitude was that you don't praise a kid too much or it'll soften him. It made for a tough environment, especially when he was often our footy coach.

I'm not blaming my father. He was just a product of his environment, of a brutal childhood and growing up suffering racism from mainstream New Zealand at a time when every Islander was called or thought of as an 'overstayer' and there were often police raids targeting Pacific Islanders. So I do understand that my old man comes from a different era and grew up in very different home circumstances. He didn't know any other way. But when you're young, growing up with an old man hardened by his own life experiences means there can be some tough moments and harsh words to bear. It is difficult to reconcile the wonderful grandad my father is to all his grandkids with the father he was when I was young. He was the father his own childhood made him. I thank my Islamic teachings for gaining that understanding about my dad, and it shows me people can change and grow.

* * *

The magic moment that first lifted me out of my neighbourhood was when the Bulldogs scout John Ackland and another scout, Mark Hughes, were watching my good mate Filinga Filiga play in a provincial league competition. I was playing in the same tournament and they liked what they saw and told me they were keen on signing me to the Bulldogs. I was fourteen.

At the time, I thought this guy was just doing me a favour because he knew my grandfather, Bill Woolsey. Pops had a big reputation. (Legend has it he was once injured and needed thirty stitches to a head wound but pushed aside the teammate who was sent on to replace him and refused to leave the game.) I was standing there, listening to this man say that he wanted me to sign with an Australian rugby league team and I was genuinely thinking it had nothing to do with me being a good player and that he was just doing it for my family. Looking back on it, I had shot up that year. Though I was still skinny as a tadpole, I reckon he looked at my big frame and could see it filled out and packing muscle one day. He was right. I went from 85 kilograms to starting my first NRL game weighing 102 kilograms.

I was in a state of disbelief after the offer, thinking I didn't really deserve to be singled out, even though I'd been chosen for the New Zealand under-16s when I was only fourteen. We went to Australia (I'm pretty sure my beautiful Nan paid my fare) and played a few games up in Queensland, where I was named Player of the Tournament. But I still thought these dudes were doing my family a favour!

Later, because Dad was working out of town, I went with my mum in her Honda Civic to go sign the Bulldogs' contract. My brother and I used to tease Mum about that car, and when she drove us to school we'd ask to be dropped off down the street so no-one would see it. Mum would do a burnout as she left to let us know what she thought of our embarrassment and to remind us we should be grateful for the lift! We quickly learned never to ask for an early drop-off.

I signed the contract on the bonnet of Mum's car. It was for a year initially and came with four payments of $250 each, so $1000 in total. It meant that the Bulldogs had the option to sign me up down the track and I was firmly on their radar. It was a lot to a fourteen-year-old! Mum and Dad said the money was supposed to go towards my schooling. Yeah, right. I drew some money out and bought a pair of Chuck Taylors. Thought I was the man walking around the neighbourhood in those. I wore them everywhere, including to school even though I wasn't supposed to.

But it wasn't just money. When you sign with an NRL club you're sent a care package, so I got a parcel full of footy boots and Bulldogs training gear. At the time, a few young guys in the area were getting picked up as NRL trainees and they'd get their packages and then walk around wearing clothing from whatever club had picked them – Parramatta, say – and other kids would see them in the club colours and ask, 'Who does this guy think he is?' I didn't want to do the wrong thing or have people think I was full of myself and boasting about my footy, so I never went outside in my Bulldogs gear. Wearing the Chuck Taylors was cool; wearing NRL colours felt boastful. Yet once on the field, my attitude was: *I'm gonna show you!*

About twelve months later, I was offered another scholarship, but with the option of either going to Sydney or staying in New Zealand till I was eighteen. Going to Sydney meant I would be training with the club and would be closer to my dream of playing first-grade NRL. In the period between the first offer and the second, a lot had changed in my game experience: I went from playing against fourteen and sixteen-year-olds to playing in the under-21s team my dad coached for the Marist Rugby League Club in Mount Albert. Johnny had been playing up in grades too, but then he'd gotten into some trouble and had to appear in court. He was sentenced to periodic detention and couldn't play footy on weekends, so it looked like Dad's team would be short. The old man asked if I wanted to play because I'd trained with them and knew them all growing up. Though I was anxious, I couldn't say yes quickly enough.

That experience of playing against men in Dad's under-21s side proved invaluable in preparing me for the big time. I matched their physicality and never showed fear on the field. I had the fitness and the ferocity to back myself every game.

One of the first times I played with the under-21s, we were up against Mount Albert, and they had some big boys in their team. Dad put me on the wing to start so I wouldn't get mangled in the forwards. This big guy runs at me and I was like, *Here we go.* I lined him up and did a massive shoulder charge. *YES!* Sure, I'd been scared playing against the men, but having the older boys in the team around me gave me the confidence not to hold back.

At half-time, Johnny rocked up as a spectator, and I spotted him on the sideline. By now, Dad had moved me in from the wing. I was in the middle, trying to mix it with the big boys, and this dude ran at me and I shoulder-charged him. Even though my arm went dead, he went flying. My brother yelled, 'Yo! That's my little brother! You just got smashed by a fifteen-year-old!'

After that game, I knew I really could mix it with the adults and that I just might have what it took to go far in this game. We ended up in the final that year and Dad picked me to start over an older player in the team, who naturally got upset at being on the bench while this skinny teenager was chosen ahead of him. I played really well and we won the competition. I might have only been fifteen and playing against men but from that moment I knew I belonged.

When he heard the options the Bulldogs had offered me, Johnny told me I should move to Sydney. I was excited by the opportunity, but I was scared of leaving my family behind. I had low self-confidence off the footy field and it always held me back and made me wary of big-noting myself. I'd never even told any of my mates that I'd been picked as a future Bulldogs player. It was that push from my brother, who I had always looked up to, that made me go. I only told a couple of my best mates I was going a day or so before I left New Zealand. One of them was Thomas Leuluai, a future Kiwi great, like his old man James Leuluai. Thomas is the only player younger than myself to play for the Kiwis. Filinga Filiga, who'd been picked up before me, injured his knee, so I travelled to Australia with Edwin Asotasi, Roy's younger brother.

* * *

I look back and I feel like I was on the edge between two worlds. On one side, I had low self-esteem – what I think of as an Islander mentality – which came from all I'd ever seen, all my father had ever seen. It was the drag that comes with the expectation of only ever filling low-income jobs, resigned to manual labour like digging holes or house painting, like my dad did. You're not supposed to ask questions; you're supposed to just shut your mouth and do as you're told. It is a fact that Māori and Pasifika kids have a higher rate of youth suicide. If you are dealing with a lack of self-belief, and that is exacerbated by the education system, higher levels of poverty and systemic racism against people of colour, then your outlook can be a negative one.

I got my right arm tattooed when I was fourteen, Sāmoan-cum-freestyle. It was to identify as Sāmoan, but it had a deeper meaning too: it was to show my individuality. But my need for that said a lot about my insecurities, my sense of not feeling good enough, even though from the outside looking in, people were perhaps thinking: *He's a cool cat. Look at him leading the way with his outrageous shoulder charges, the offloads, the running – and now he's got his own version of a traditional Sāmoan tattoo.* But, really, it was more about putting that mask on, a plaster over the internal bleeding of not truly loving myself. In class, I kept my shirt sleeve rolled down over the tatt, but outside the classroom I rolled up my sleeve and proudly showed it off.

In my family, there had always been a sense of being kept down, which must have fed from when they brought Sāmoans over to New Zealand in the 1960s to do all the shitty jobs: the mind-numbing factory work; the low-paid night shifts as cleaners. They lost their connection to land and mostly lived in urban areas. I had to wrestle against that in-built mentality in order to believe I could do and be anything. I didn't think I could do anything except sport. On the rugby field, I was the boss. I had to tell myself I had the best job, not the shittiest. I was smashing guys four to six years older than me, and I could actually shine.

Before I was offered the chance to move to Australia, my mate and I set up a homemade gym with discards from his older brother but we had no idea what we were doing. I look back now, laughing. We used old breeze blocks as weights to bench press and we'd take turns holding the bricks in place so they didn't fall off while the other worked out. It was a mad buzz and we'd pump hard thinking we were Ronnie Coleman, who was crowned Mr Olympia eight years running. We were trying to improve ourselves. I'd go for road runs, not knowing why except that it helped feed my confidence – I knew that was necessary if I was to really succeed. When I was a young kid I was good at athletics, but by about ten or eleven I would watch NRL on television and think, *If I can play footy on TV it means I am successful.* From then on, footy seemed a pathway to success for me, and the symbol of that success was being able to buy my mum a house.

I grew up living in state housing in Mount Albert, a working-class suburb of Auckland. A lot of the houses had been built in the fifties and sixties and many were double-storey, packed side by side. You could almost always hear what was happening in the neighbours' houses. My parents were paying low or subsidised rent, but it meant the house was never truly ours. My mum and dad lived pay cheque to pay cheque so could never get ahead, but I knew Mum dreamed of owning her own home one day. The house we lived in was run-down and there were places where you could see there had, at one time, been wallpaper on the walls but it had been stripped off. There were remnants here and there that showed what had been. I had this thought fixed in my mind: *I'm going to buy Mum a house one day – a house with fancy wallpaper.* I couldn't see that happening through education. I knew that school was not for me. *Stuff school, what has it ever done for my family?* So, sport was the only way.

I'd get out there and do shoulder charges and make spectacular offloads, all this amazing stuff on the paddock, and I'd slap down my low self-esteem for a while. At the same time, I held back when we weren't playing, in the club house or sheds or at training, because I didn't want to step on anyone's toes or say or do the wrong thing. If anyone of higher social status or in a position of authority spoke to me, I was like, 'Yes, sir.'

If I was asked to say a few words after a match, my mouth would go dry. I didn't feel like my voice counted or that I had the knowledge to speak up. I was this fair-skinned Sāmoan and never felt like I owned my own space or place in the world.

I sometimes struggle even now, despite all the success in four different sports. For so long I'd thought, *Who needs education to succeed?* I didn't see a pathway for my family or myself through education, and I saw how the system let down those who didn't have money or status. But that has changed. Through my experiences in life, I have learned the value and power that comes from knowledge and I have experienced the naivety one can have without it. From my own growth, and to show my kids sport isn't the only avenue for success, I went back to school and enrolled in a Bachelor of Applied Management through Capable New Zealand, a school within Otago Polytechnic. That was a big thing for me, but I've learned that you can find empowerment through understanding history. Knowing your people's history can give you the confidence to go to any level of society, to enter any room and be articulate, talk your talk and stand up for what you believe in instead of being held back by the expectation that the Pacific Islander or Māori is either meant to stay silent or make people laugh.

* * *

When I went over to Sydney, I was still the young bloke who mostly kept his thoughts to himself, worried I would say the wrong thing or show I didn't understand something. A guy named Garry Carden trained all the young Bulldogs guys at Belmore. Garry was at the club for thirty-seven years all up, before leaving in 2020. He looked after so many of us and made sure we trained hard. His conditioning helped me put on that seventeen kilos. His dedication and expertise definitely prepared me to step up and shaped my career in the important early days.

> I've been lucky enough to train the two best players that have played for Canterbury in the modern era in Sonny Bill Williams and Johnathan Thurston. Sonny is the best athlete I've ever trained. He was just a big, tall, skinny kid when he arrived. But he used to do a lot of things that other kids never did. He was always doing stuff on a balance beam and the rest is history, of course. People see Sonny's work ethic now, but we give them that work ethic when they come to the Dogs. – Garry Carden

Training and working out in the gym was easy. I knew exactly what I had to do by then and did it. It was the other stuff that was harder to navigate. I was supposed to enrol in a high school, but I wanted to work, because I thought that was the quickest way to make it into the team. On that first visit, I worked and trained for eight weeks and then went home for two weeks. Once back in Auckland, I didn't want to return to Australia because I knew I'd miss my family too much. I loved being back home with them, my mates and especially my mum. I didn't want to leave. But I knew deep down that the only way I could make something of myself and buy Mum that house with fancy wallpaper was to go back to the big smoke in Australia. My old man kicked my arse, but I was pretty driven to try to make it for my family on my own, because we didn't have much. Still, leaving them for the second time was even worse than the first. It was such a massive thing for a fifteen-year-old to do. I was going back to a place without family or close mates. It was really tough. I trained hard in Sydney, but I had no-one to confide in, no-one I felt I could tell how lonely I was. I was too shy to admit how homesick I felt. I would lie in bed, staring at the ceiling, unable to sleep because I felt so homesick. The only thing I knew I could do to distract myself was train hard and push myself physically, so by the time night came I was hopefully too tired to feel. It didn't always work and so I would stare at the ceiling and wait for the sun to come up again. It was a really trying time.

Back in Sydney, I again had the choice of work or school, but I found out going to school would delay my NRL debut, so I got a job labouring on a building site, digging holes and carrying stuff. I went from training twice a week and playing touch footy with my mates back home to working full-time as a labourer and training professionally. I'd leave the house in the dark and get back in the dark. Along with nine other scholarship boys, I lived with a couple named Mary and Peter Durose in what was called the 'Bulldogs House', but as much as they looked out for us all, it wasn't home.

I did that labouring for a while and then I got a job in an embroidery factory, where I was the storeman out the back, while dreaming only of running out onto the field with the premier NRL Canterbury Bulldogs team. But while that wouldn't happen for a couple of years, I did at least manage to graduate from the storeman job to something more linked to footy.

As far as my playing went, I was really starting to hit my straps and made the Canterbury-Bankstown under-18s SG Ball Cup team, competing against all the major NRL clubs, barring Queensland. It was a real big deal. I was now training like a full-time professional and being part of that set-up took my game to another level. That improvement would see me named Player of the Tournament. For a shy fella a long way from home, this was a huge boost to my self-esteem. It also led to the Bulldogs bringing me closer to their home ground by giving me a job doing all sorts of tasks at the club. As soon as I'd finished my work, I could go sit in the grandstand and watch the guys train. It was heaven! Watching stars like Matt Utai, Hazem El Masri, Mark O'Meley, the Hughes brothers, Steve Price, Brent Sherwin, Nigel Vagana and Willie Mason right there in front of me, showing me how to train and play hard. I knew one day soon my turn was coming.

Matty, Nigel and Willie asked me, the kid, how I was, did I need anything? Man, it is something else to get acknowledgement from guys like that when you are a young fella. These guys really made me feel special. I have taken this lesson with me, and I always try to make sure the young guys are heard and seen.

I first met Sonny just after I signed with the Bulldogs. I remember going to training on my day off and driving through the car park at Belmore and seeing two young fellas sitting on the ground on the edge of the car park near the fire exit. As I drove past, I gave the Kiwi wave . . . two eyebrows up, and they both returned the wave. I then noticed a tattoo on the forearm of one of the guys and so recognised them as Island boys.

I got out of the car and walked over to them. They were two young brothers who looked lost. I asked what they were up to.

'Just waiting for training,' the one without the tattoo said.

'What time's training?'

'Six pm.'

I looked at my watch and saw it was 4 pm. 'Man, you guys are early. You from New Zealand?'

'Yeah, bro, Auckland. I'm from South, he's from Central.'

'Ah, sweet. I'm from Central too. I'm Nigel.'

'Oh, hey. I'm Edwin [Asotasi].'

'I'm Sonny.'

'You guys Sāmoan?' I asked.

'Yep.'

Sonny came across as quiet. Street smart, tough, didn't say much, but what he said he meant. I would come to learn that, above all, he was loyal. Would stay and fight to the end with you. He always wanted to protect . . . a trait I still see in him today. When I walked over from the car, I thought about what it felt like when I arrived in Sydney as a twenty-five-year-old. I knew how these guys might be feeling. All I wanted to do was check that the young brothers were okay and let them know if they needed anything, I was there for them. – Nigel Vagana

I used to make sure I got through everything I was supposed to do in the morning so I could then spend time watching the guys in my position, see what they did. Even though a lot of it was new, I just soaked up everything. The cool thing was I got on really well with the gear steward; he was Italian and his name was Fred Ciraldo.

Freddie had been with the club for years and he looked after me, taught me the ins and outs of the club. Freddie would often tell his boss he needed me to help him out, so I'd be there helping him on the field and then one day Steve Folkes, the coach, came over and said a couple of guys had injuries. 'Can you come and stand in?' he asked me. You bet I could!

That session turned into invites to train with the first-grade team, even if I was just holding the tackle bags. I loved it. Two years before, I'd been playing with my brother in teams my dad coached, and now here I was at sixteen in the company of these illustrious footy stars. The first-grade players were kind to me. There were no big egos, no 'I'm too busy and important to interact with the rookie' stuff. I thought they were all lovely guys, really good dudes who were always happy to chat to me. They could have said to me, 'Take my dirty laundry home and wash it and bring it back neatly folded' and I would have been happy to oblige.

* * *

Being on the edge of the team like that meant I was laying the foundations for my debut game. I would see what they were doing and go away and work on my skills. I'd train with them in the morning, then train either alone or with my age-group peers in the late afternoon and into the evening. The one thing I didn't imitate or copy was their drinking. I didn't touch alcohol. The other scholarship boys all drank hard; I was the only one who didn't indulge. Yet no-one, not one person, ever pressured me to drink.

Growing up, there was a lot of love in the house, but my old man drank quite a bit and it made things pretty volatile, which put me off alcohol. I now understand my father was drinking and gambling, trying to bury the pain from a tough upbringing with extremely violent uncles after his mother abandoned him at the age of ten. He didn't talk about it when I was young, so I didn't know much about what he'd been through. I remember the old man and his mates drinking at the club. It was like that *Once Were Warriors* boozing scene. I remember him actually belting a man for slapping his partner in the club rooms. That violence was normal to him. It was what he knew. Though he never laid a hand on Mum, us kids often walked on eggshells in case he lost his temper with us – Johnny especially.

Even though Dad's brothers were bikies, they were a close family. When they came round to our home, their boots would all be lined up out on the front doorstep and all these big, fierce dudes would be sitting quietly and respectfully inside while my little Pākehā mum,

Lee, cooked them a big feed. Stereotypes are made to be broken!

We had a real stroppy redneck neighbour who the old man had a row with one time because our dog was barking. Dad was trying to talk to him and the neighbour told him he was a black coconut and that he should shut the dog up before he did. Dad was smart enough not to jump the fence and have it out with him, as he'd be the one arrested for trespass with violent intent, or whatever the charge is. But Mum called my bikie uncles, who didn't care about the consequences of jumping over some redneck's fence. Luckily, the guy took off at seeing these hulking Sāmoan gangies turn up.

If I hadn't become a professional sportsman, I could have easily wound up selling drugs, hustling, maybe ended up in prison. Sport has saved many like me.

* * *

Instead of starting me in the under-20s season when I was seventeen, the Bulldogs put me straight into reserve grade, playing against men – hard, experienced, fully grown men, some of them ready to knock my block off. I more than held my own and was playing really well and made the New South Wales under-19s side – but then injury struck. I was scoring a try and popped my shoulder out. I tried to play on but I knew I had done something bad. I had to have a shoulder reconstruction and was out for the rest of the year. This was my first real experience of injury impacting my career, but I managed to keep focused and not let the depression overwhelm me too much. I just had to get it sorted.

Mark Hughes picked me up from the Bulldog House and took me for my surgery. On the way home after the op, he said to me, 'I've got some good news. You've been picked in the top twenty-five for next year.'

That knowledge took my mind off my shoulder! For a start, it meant I'd go from earning ten grand a year to forty-five grand. I would be rich! I could buy my mum that house! I was so ecstatic, it actually got me through my misery at being out with injury for so long and I worked hard on my fitness and rehab to make sure I made that team.

My shoulder had healed by the time the 2004 pre-season training started. I was still very shy, but because I'd been working at the club for a year and knew some of the guys, it was not such a massive step up physically. However, mentally it saw me struggling with the two sides of myself – the confidence I displayed on the field was the complete opposite once I stepped off the ground.

That pre-season training was as I expected: really, really hard. But I loved almost every moment. When the coach told me he was starting me at centre for the trials, straight away I put on the bravado. *Yo, I'm sweet.* Inside, I was in turmoil. The self-doubt is always there and I started to doubt myself and ask myself if I was really ready. When I was training or playing I was okay, but at night I would lie there worrying, scared I'd blow it. Make a fool of myself or, worse than that, let down my teammates. I was constantly wrestling with myself and that internal conflict can be pretty exhausting. In the end, I would learn to drown out the negative feelings and focus on the positive, but it didn't mean the doubts left me. I just prepared hard so I could walk with them.

Who was I marking in that first game? In the first half I was up against the Australian centre, Mark Gasnier. The second half I marked Matt Cooper. Yet again, I held my own. I stood up Cooper one time. I stood him up and did an outside-in. Gasnier didn't get around me at all and he was the best attacking centre at the time. Although it was only a trial, as a now eighteen-year-old holding his own against the best in the world, it gave me huge confidence.

I remember as a kid watching my dad play and here I was doing the same thing, real aggressive; I almost had a fight with Matt Cooper. After that game I knew for sure that I definitely had what it took to play in this league.

Two weeks later I was named in the starting Bulldogs side at centre for the season's first game. I was so excited, so nervous. Remember, I'm only eighteen. But on the day, my only thought was to make my family proud. Pity about the forgotten boots! Well, that was the only blemish on the most unforgettable day of my young life.

Waking up the next morning and seeing my performance written about and spoken of in the media in the most complimentary terms was overwhelming. In the back of my mind I was thinking, *If only they knew how shy I am, what low self-esteem I have.* That massive outpouring of praise was a lot to deal with.

Four games after that and my name was read out as a New Zealand international in the Kiwis team. I still remember the phone call. What a feeling! I was to become the second youngest to represent New Zealand behind my good mate Tommy Leuluai. That is big! Us boys from the same hood, who went to the same school and who grew up together, both achieving a feat like that was really special.

I played pretty well in my first Test against Australia. The next Bulldogs game was against Souths, and I came off the bench only to be injured and was out for ten weeks. Injury rendered me helpless and, to my mind, my life kind of meaningless. That's the first time I experienced a serious depression I found hard to shake, for what was I – *who* was I – if I couldn't play footy?

After the time out, and putting my effort into rehab, I was put into reserve grade. I played really well, and the coach called me back into the premier team, and I then had a great run of playing every game well.

People talk a lot about my talent, but my success on the field only comes about from hard work beforehand. I've always been a dedicated trainer who takes no shortcuts; in fact, I'm more likely to do the opposite, taking on extra training, doubling up on repetition exercises and hard aerobics, trying new things and always pushing myself. Maybe my low self-esteem, my never thinking I was good enough, pushed me to train that much harder. I know they say practice makes perfect, but does it really? Personally, I have never been able to visit that room of perfection. I guess I know I'll never be able to, but the inspiration I get from striving to be my best is what I love. My best as a player, sure, but it is more than that. I strive to be a better person both on and off the field. So as far as footy goes, I did everything asked of me and then some.

The offloads are a perfect example. It started when I was young, maybe ten or eleven, trying flash things in the backyard with Johnny, or with my mates, or on the school oval, then putting them to the test in a game. To see one come off for the first time only makes you work harder at perfecting the pass

In the backyard I started off trying big hits with my brother, my mates and even my little twin sisters, Niall and Denise! Although I held back a bit with my sisters, the practice might have done them a good turn; Niall ended up captain of the New Zealand touch team and won Olympic silver with the New Zealand rugby sevens.

> Growing up with two older brothers – Sonny is three years older and Johnny five years – I looked up to them, wanted to hang out with them and do whatever they were doing. Older siblings are often too cool for the younger ones, but they were both good to me and my sister Denise. They let us join in their footy games and backyard cricket. One of them would come racing down the driveway and bowl me out then do the same to Denise. The penalty for being bowled out was we had to feed them, like slaves, for hours. 'Niall, get me this.' 'Denise, can you get me . . .' We'd play footy in the lounge room; our brothers would go down on their knees and we had to score a try past them. We got smashed, absolutely smashed. But we loved it. – Niall Williams

For me, it was about proving myself by smashing the big guys (never my sisters!). That's how the shoulder charge came about. Remember, I had a point to prove to other Islanders: that even though I was a fair-skinned Sāmoan, I was still one of them and this was how I'd prove it.

* * *

It is strange. When we started working on this book, Alan asked me to recall my childhood. At first I couldn't think of anything significant – not until my wife reminded me of an event so significant it helped define my life. After I told her about it, I must have blanked it out, again parking the memory in some dark corner of my mind.

In New Zealand, there's an organisation called the Plunket Society which offers services to promote the health and wellbeing of kids under five. Registered nurses known as 'Plunket nurses' would come round to help mothers feed and care for babies. Given that Mum had twin girls to look after as well as two older boys also needing attention, a Plunket nurse suggested Mum drop one of us off at Barnardos – a charity dedicated to providing care and support for children and families in need – to give her a break. Lee Williams was a very protective mum, and when she took the nurse's advice and sent me there at four years old, she trusted that I would be looked after. I was in the backyard of the Barnados residence playing with the kid of the woman who ran the place. Two teenagers were in the kitchen cooking chips when the fat erupted in flames. One of them ran outside with the pot and, depending on who you ask, either threw it without watching where it was going or it exploded.

Whatever happened, the result was I ended up with boiling fat down the backs of my legs. I guess one reason

I've blanked it out all this time is the pain. It's a kind of pain only someone who's been severely burnt can understand. The other kid only got a few drops of hot fat on him, yet his mother scooped him up, ran inside and put him into the bath, which she filled with cold water. In the meantime, yours truly was left outside alone, screaming his head off. Luckily, the neighbours were washing their car and, hearing the commotion, jumped over the fence and hosed me down. Without their quick thinking, the result would have been catastrophic.

I spent six to eight months, maybe longer, in the intensive burns unit at Auckland City Hospital. When my parents came to visit, the doctors forbade them to touch me because the skin grafts were so fragile, and they needed to stretch and become elastic. Mum still cries when she tells this story, even thirty years later.

When we went to see Sonny Bill at the hospital, they would get him to walk to us but when he tried he'd fall to the ground and start screaming for us to pick him up. I would go to help him but his dad would have to pull me away because we'd been told to leave him. He would be crawling and looking at us. It was the most horrific thing to look at your kid in that much agony, crawling along the ground and just saying, 'Why aren't you helping me?' They said if we picked him up and carried him, the skin wouldn't stretch and he wouldn't be able to walk.

When he came home, my wee boy, just four years old, was in a wheelchair, a sight to break any mother's heart. We had to give him baths and his skin kept coming off and we had to do the bathing as part of the healing process. Oh, how that child suffered, and his parents with him. – Lee Williams

Mum put on a brave face but she was dying inside and bawled her eyes out after every visit. I do have memories of incredible pain. The healing process took several more months, during which time Mum had to unbandage me and rub a special cream on my legs.

When I had finally healed, I started school, where a different kind of pain was waiting.

Because of my scars, the kids there called me 'Kentucky Fried Chicken legs' or 'SBL' (Sonny Burnt Legs), and that stuck with me my whole life. It shaped my childhood a lot. I was always really self-conscious, and I reckon it just added to my poor self-esteem. It was a very, very tough time.

It was worse at intermediate school, because as I got older I became more worried about what other people thought, and of course the self-consciousness got worse. My first day there, I was wearing shorts and I remember everyone staring at my legs. It was bad enough being half-Sāmoan and having a pale complexion without the stares as well.

From then on, I wore long pants, even on boiling-hot days. On weekends, playing footy, I had to wear shorts and my legs were so white – and scarred – it felt like they glowed. I remember one time I put fake tan on them; I was running around with legs the colour of Donald Trump's face!

I think the burns had a huge psychological effect on me. Growing up, I had a lot of demons from that. But I think I turned that on its head, too; I was determined to make those skinny white legs muscly. Maybe it made me train harder? I do sometimes think about the effect of those burns on the person I became. When I talked about it with Alan Duff for this book, he suggested that the experience took me to the edge of the pain barrier, which means I can push myself harder at training than others can. He may have a point; even if the memory is buried, the knowledge is there.

Later, aged twenty-one and playing for the Bulldogs, I got the whole back of my right leg tattooed. (My left leg wasn't as scarred.) Later, I'd run into young guys – white guys, Anglos – who had the exact same tattoo, copied from shots of my tatt. I've heard getting tattooed over scar tissue is particularly painful. I'd have to agree with that. My leg was so sore, and I had it done in one eight-hour sitting. But I was so excited at finally being able to wear shorts and not feel bad that I was prepared to cop the pain.

* * *

Before the tatts, before I started making a name for myself in footy, I was down at our primary school playing on the monkey bars one Sunday, just for something to do. There's an Islander church next to the school and some big Island kids came over and slapped me around. I went back home and told Mum what happened.

As I said, my mum is very protective, and she goes, 'Right. Let's go!'

We marched down to the church, and I stood in the doorway hanging back as she walked in.

I marched in and these Islanders are thinking, *Who is this crazy Palangi woman interrupting our church service?*

They tell me, 'Excuse me, but the pastor is speaking. Are you okay, lady?'

'No. I'm not okay. My kid was playing at the school and some big, older kids came and gave him a hiding. Now, I don't know what kind of God you believe in, but to me that's not what God teaches, giving smaller kids a hiding.'

This is in the middle of the sermon and everyone stops.

'I'm coming back here next Sunday, and I want you to find out who did this and make them apologise to my son.'

At home, later, my husband John is going off at me. How dare I, a white woman, walk into an Islander church like that? But I didn't care. When I'm in the right, nothing stops me.

The next Sunday, John drives me, John Arthur and Sonny
Bill to the church. But even though he's a tough Sāmoan who
doesn't take shit, John ain't going into that church and nor is
John junior.

I did. And I came out with the guilty kids, who apologised to
Sonny Bill. – Lee Williams

This white, red-haired, freckled lady who believed in
doing the right thing no matter the consequences taught
me a lot. I hope that, like her, I will never budge, not
even for an army, when it comes to my principles.
A classic example of this is when I left the Bulldogs
in 2008. Maybe if, at the time, I had more confidence
to speak out and discuss the issues I was wrestling
with, things would have been different. But I didn't
know how. There was so much speculation about why
I walked out and none of it comes close to the real
reason. It wasn't about contract dramas or money or
playing another code. The truth was, I was losing my
sense of self and had lost sight of that fire my old lady
gave to me. I know what is right and what is wrong, but
I was losing the ability to only walk towards the good.
Physically I was okay but mentally my head was in a
bad place. I thought running away was my only option.
At the time, I didn't realise you can't run away from the
man in the mirror, and nothing I did was going to stop

a confrontation with him, with myself. But right then, I had to do something or else I truly believed I'd be lost – to alcohol or to drugs or to a dangerous situation I couldn't handle or survive.

CHAPTER 2

Dressing a deep wound with sticking plaster

In our house, no-one could have loved us more than our mum. She stuck up for her kids and made us feel good about ourselves. Dad loved us in his way, but he didn't show it like Mum. I'm not judging my father; he'd had a tough life and he'd had to adapt just to survive. He took a big interest in our sports, and we knew we made him proud, but he'd never been taught to love unconditionally.

When I got older, I could see where Mum's love came from: her mum, our wonderful Nan, a woman I miss greatly. Such a beautiful lady. She was a little woman whose Australian sense of humour we found a bit weird till we got to know her style. She was always singing, laughing and teasing us and she loved having us around. Her house was often the meeting place for our family;

she was a welcoming, loving woman who loved a chat. Pop, on the other hand, was this gruff, unapproachable man of few words; we'd heard he was a real tough guy who would punch other men out. We never got to know him because he didn't want to know us. He ignored us kids and we didn't dare upset him. He and Nan were chalk and cheese.

Neither of our houses had much by way of food – unless Dad had a good win on the horses – but Nan always had a few lollies or some ice cream for us kids. The first thing we did when we got to her place was check out the fridge for treats. There'd be chocolate broken into small pieces to make it last longer. Our favourite lollies. To us it meant everything, as we hardly got sweet treats at home.

As kids, Sonny Bill was the one with the self-control. While the rest of us scoffed our ice cream or iceblock as soon as we got it, he put his in the freezer box then would pull it out later and eat it in front of us really slowly, laughing at our envy. I think he might have felt sorry for us, though, because he always gave us a lick or two. – Niall Williams

I can confirm what Niall said about Sonny having self-control. But while I remember watching him eat his saved iceblock, I have no memory of him giving me so much as a single lousy lick! – Denise Williams

On the weekends, either my twin sisters or me and my older brother Johnny would stay on at Nan's after the family visit. There'd be some pretty heavy sadness if you were the one who had to ride home in Mum's Honda Civic, because those who stayed could look forward to a day and night of luxury. It might mean going into town with Nan on the bus, playing *Space Invaders*, going to a movie and having ice creams before heading home to more sweet treats. Man, that was like gold for us. At bedtime she would rub Vicks VapoRub into our chests and then turn on the electric blanket. That was the height of luxury!

I was lucky to have such fiercely loving women in my life. And they would both stick up for us kids in an instant. Like I said, Dad was different. Mum's got some strong thoughts about Dad's family and why he struggled as a parent:

For a few years, some of John's family didn't like me – I guess because I was white. My mum and dad didn't give two hoots that he was Sāmoan, just as long as he looked after me and I was happy. That's all my mum cared about: that he took care of me like she had.

When they had a funeral in his large family, everyone was expected to give money and quite a lot. John's mum was pretty demanding. I'd tell her we couldn't afford it; we had our own little

47

kids to look after. I'd say, 'The person we're giving the money to is a relation of a relation of a relation I don't even know.' Money to feed the mourners and leave nothing to feed my own kids? To hell with that. It had nothing to do with me being white. I was just making sure I looked after our children first. So many Islanders get into financial trouble trying to meet this social obligation. They worry about what other family members will think if they don't contribute. Not this little white lady! I look after my own kids first.

Was I intimidated by them? No way! I didn't care if there was a hundred of them; I'd take them all on if I knew I was right. I wasn't just a little Pākehā girl you could walk all over.

If you are doing something right, you always know it is right. If I'm doing something good and fair dinkum about it, I'll keep going all the way to the end. But when you know you're doing something wrong, you get a bit hesitant, a bit lost, and think, *Yeah, maybe I am in the wrong here.* I told my kids: 'If you do something wrong, then just admit it. It's not the end of the world.'

Because of suicide and all that, I used to say to them, 'I just want you to know that I don't give two hoots if you've done the worst thing in the whole wide world. I want you always to know the door's still wide open, and we might not be able to fix it, but we will talk about it and try to make it as good as we can. You will be getting a kick up the backside and not getting away with it, but never think you can't come home, because nothing is ever that bad that your own home is closed to you.'

My mum [Sonny Bill's Nan] was unbelievably nice. One of those real Aussies, just cracking jokes and always finding the brighter side to life. She used to live in Paddington, in Sydney, back when it was a rough area, not posh and expensive like it is now. Six kids living in a two-bedroom terrace house. Her dad, my grandad, went up the road one day to get a loaf of bread and never came back. Left Gran with six kids having to top and tail in beds. I suppose that's where Mum got her humour from. You have to look on the bright side of life, even when it's pitch-black and miserable. She gave me that outlook and I tried to pass it on to my kids. I think they all turned out pretty damn good.

Mum met my Kiwi dad while he was playing league in Sydney. They moved to Auckland in 1957 and lived in a flat they said was terrible. I wasn't born yet. They asked Housing Corp for a house to rent. When they said they didn't have any available, my dad went, 'Righto, we're leaving our kids here with you. We are not taking them back to that scummy flat we're living in.' The Housing Corp people scurried around and next thing we knew, we were living in a very nice house reserved for their senior managers right near the beach in Westmere — another suburb that's now flash, where houses sell for a couple of million and more.

I met John down at my father's club, City Newton Rugby League, when I was still at high school. He sat behind me and when I got up, I accidentally moved my chair onto his foot. We got talking and we liked each other straight away. He later told me other people had said, *'Do you know whose daughter that is? Bill Woolsey's.'* John didn't care.

John Arthur and Sonny Bill were born before John and I married. — Lee Williams

* * *

I can't remember the exact moment the thought formed of buying Mum a house one day. Maybe it was knowing her and Nan's histories. And because I wanted to see her live in a place with fancy wallpaper that was all her own. All I really know is, the older I got, and with my sport improving all the time, that dream got stronger. I could make it happen when I was only a young man playing NRL, and it felt so good.

I would encourage young Pacific Islanders and Māori to get hold of a dream like that and never let it go. Because dreams can and do come true. And sporting success is not the only way; there are all kinds of businesses and professional careers and trades you can get into. There's nothing to stop you from claiming one of those career choices and just going for it.

I wish I had a magic wand to wave self-belief into our Pasifika and Māori youngsters, since we have the most catching up to do. I see now so much untapped potential;

it's like a human diamond mine waiting to be discovered – by ourselves.

Everyone can have dreams beyond your own little world. And dreams evolve depending on what stage of life you are at. My dreams as a young bloke were to play in the NRL and to buy my mum a house. Then they changed into playing with the All Blacks. Each time you achieve a dream, it is important to reflect and create a new goal. Now my dreams are to be the best husband and best father and family man I can be. I want to be a spokesperson for my people and to give a voice to those who can't speak up for themselves. If you had told me twenty years ago I would be standing up for refugees and trying to speak with the Australian prime minister about asylum-seeker policy, I would have laughed at you. But I have evolved, learned and kept trying to honour the spark my mum ignited in me.

Life really does boil down to an attitude. And succeeding isn't measured by money or status; it can be doing something well. Being the best you can be. My attitude to sport helped me achieve because I recognised the importance of training hard all the time with no let-up. When I least felt like training, that was all the more reason to get out there and do it. Sleeping in was not an option. Being really fit allows you to do more in a game, because your lungs are not gasping for air, your brain is clearer. A very fit player can compensate for having less talent than a lazy one. I was lucky I carried that attitude my whole life. However it may have looked from the outside, I always valued hard work and never tried to coast on talent alone.

It's funny how my flamboyant style of play made me look to some like a self-confident extrovert. I definitely was not that when off the field; you could hardly get boo out of me. That perceived flamboyance in my early days and right up to my mid-twenties did not go down well in rugby union and rugby league circles. The two codes had a conventional attitude, a set of fixed game plans that coaches sternly instructed players to follow. As I got older, I'd always question things and say what I thought I could do better or what the coach could do better. For some reason, when it came to rugby league, I wasn't scared to express my opinions. But it took years for me to get to that point and only came when I let myself believe I knew what I was talking about.

I did write everything down and try to stick to the coach's game plan. But I did best when I just went out there and played. I worked so hard training, put so much effort into every game, and I would stick to the structures as best I could. I prided myself on making the two-tackles double, getting up and reloading fast, doing the grind work. That was the glue that held everything together –

doing your job and a little bit more. Then could come the flavour, the specialness.

When it comes to coaches, you can have great ones and you can have less than great ones. But no matter how good a coach might be, if they don't have talent to work with, they ain't got nothing. I think we get too caught up in this idea that the coach is more important than the players. In reality, it's the players who bring the majority of what you need to win a game, and then the consistency – and attitude – to win a competition. A true coach is more of a people manager; he (or she) understands the different backgrounds of individual players, understands how to get the best out of each one, how to bring them together as a team. Yes, structure is needed. But the coach is only one element in a team of players and reserves. And remember, it's the players, not the coach, who actually go out and play. If I mess up, it's not my coach's fault. A good coach can bring out magic, and I have had some amazing coaches do that; I'll introduce you to a few of them later in the book. Game plans and tactics are important, but you've got to have the skills to draw on.

Thinking about my parents and talking about structure makes me realise something. I think my dad's problem is he had no structure to his life. Brought up by his grandmother and his uncles, he'd never been given that. He was a very hard worker, a real good player in his day, and a stand-out coach throughout the age groups. Like I said, Dad grew up in a brutal environment of countless beatings from uncles who were all boxers. To see him now as the most loving, consistent grandad is to understand that you can outgrow a rough childhood. But you can't know what you don't know; everyone understands that. I think lumping everyone into one group and expecting them to react the same way is not realistic. We are all different and react differently. To be a good coach, you have to understand the individuals on your team and help to bring out the best in them in a tailored way.

* * *

The burns I suffered as a four-year-old were just the beginning. On the injury count, Mum tells me I was dropped on my head as a baby by one of my teenage cousins and fractured my skull. Dad saw my head swelling and raced me to hospital, breaking every speed limit ever invented.

So it is possible that my experience of spills, burns, breaks and infections may have given me the means to endure all my league and rugby injuries. Another painful memory was when I was nine years old and got tackled. Then several of the opposition boys were punching me in the back. I just got up and kept playing. The next day, my back really hurt. Mum took me to hospital and next minute, I was in intensive care getting a needle in my spine and the blood drained from a big sac that had formed on my lower back. I'd got infected where they punched me, and it was so bad I could have died. Poor Mum ground her teeth for years over that one, wishing she'd been at the game so she could have given my assailants a slap around the ears!

I hadn't played more than twenty games with the Bulldogs before I got injured and had a long stint on the sidelines. Although the injury would heal, the dark place I'd find myself in would not be as easily fixed.

I was defined by the game of rugby league and for a young fella from Auckland who had dreamed of playing NRL, the thought of this dream evaporating was devastating. The season before I had been named the Rugby League International Federation (RLIF) Rookie of the Year and the same in the Rugby League Players Association (RLPA) awards. And I had earned the respect of some people I really admire, like Graham Lowe, who was the Kiwis coach from 1983 to 1986 as well as the coach of numerous international clubs. He was quoted in the *NZ Herald*:

During my coaching career I was fortunate enough to have guided three of the best of all time – Mark Graham, Ellery Hanley and

Wally Lewis. I don't say it lightly, but I think Williams will turn out to be better than each of them.

Williams, who has just turned nineteen, has already received numerous accolades. Canberra Raiders great Laurie Daley has been really impressed by his talent and is in no doubt he will be New Zealand's greatest.

But none of that mattered if I couldn't play. I have no memory of being complimented by the great man himself at the time. I'm flattered and humbled, but if people could have seen into my mind, they'd have been aware how unprepared I was for all that acclaim and how much I struggled to deal with the setbacks of injury. Just about every person who finds success young goes through the same thing: your immature mind is not equipped to deal with that fame and those stresses.

I could feel a nagging inner pain that I couldn't put my finger on. In fact, I looked the other way. I truly believed I was a better person because I was a good footy player. Turning nineteen and getting paid a truckload of money and being showered in praise by the media and rugby league commentators, including former great players and coaches. You'd think it was every young man's dream – till it happens to you.

Don't get me wrong. It didn't go to my head straight away; I was still shy. But in the back of my mind I could sense something major changing. Winning and starring in an NRL grand final might have been a highlight, but I was only four years away from a personal crisis – not as a player, but as a human being. I was being praised to the skies, but those words didn't heal my inner self. Inside, I was deeply unhappy.

* * *

That first season was also my first experience with alcohol. To begin with, I hated the taste – and I hated the hangover even more. Going out with the boys to pubs, I couldn't really handle people coming up and telling me how great I was, buying me drinks. *Who, me?* Suddenly, the shy Islander boy standing outside the nightclub was getting called to the front of the queue. People would be shaking my hand, patting me on the back. It messed with me.

My first time in a nightclub, I went to the bar to buy a round of drinks and I had no idea what to do. I ordered bourbon and Cokes for my teammates, two each. A beautiful woman introduced herself while I was at the bar. She said, 'I saw you interviewed on television and saw how shy you are. I find that really appealing.' I kind of stumbled my way through the conversation.

We talked for a while and then she said, 'Aren't you going to invite me home?' As a naive teenager, that was my introduction to the world of women.

The league culture was train hard and play hard – and then party hard. When it came to alcohol, I was a very late starter. I'd seen the damage it could do. But it didn't stop me.

* * *

One day, not all that long before I moved to Australia, Mum took me aside to say she and Dad had split up. Niall, Denise and Johnny were staying with Mum, but I chose to stay with Dad because I didn't like the idea of him living alone.

Six months later, Johnny was living with his girlfriend and selling drugs out of his rented house. It is strange even saying that, because it is so far away from the man he is today. Johnny is now a Muslim, the proud dad of six kids, happily married, and he doesn't touch drugs or alcohol. But back then, things weren't good.

Funny thing, when I got offered the Dogs scholarship, my old man stopped treating me like a boy and started treating me like a man he respected. He had a second run-around car that he let me drive. I didn't even have a licence! Dad's cousin, who we called Uncle Ben even though technically he was our second cousin, came to stay with us and he was on the dole. In the mornings, I'd put on my school uniform so my father could see me heading off to school, drive around the block and wait until Dad left for work, and then come back and be on PlayStation all day with Ben. Then I'd put my school uniform back on for when Dad came home so he thought I was a good lad. But Dad was much harder on Johnny and never made it easy for him.

My brother was my hero growing up. He had a reputation for being one of the hardest players on a footy field and he didn't mind a fight. I was more withdrawn and wasn't really into fighting as a youngster. I didn't get into many fights throughout my long career in the three footy codes either. It might seem a bit ironic then that I became a boxer.

I stopped going to school because I knew I had the Dogs scholarship coming up. Like I said earlier, school had never really interested me. I think I said in one interview that I was no rocket scientist. I also had that chip on my shoulder about getting an education. For me, it was all about footy.

I had a bad feeling when I stopped seeing my brother Johnny at school. I remember an incident while he was still at school; we were at a bus stop and Johnny went off to a petrol station to buy some smokes for himself, and this kid across the street, walking along with two girls, gave me the evils. I didn't even know him. Next thing I knew, he came over to confront me. I was really scared about what he would do.

Then Johnny arrived and flew at the dude and they got into it. After Johnny dropped the guy a third time, he got up and pointed a finger at us both then walked off. I won't name names, but this guy would end up becoming a professional boxer.

I had a feeling he would come back with some dudes and was thinking, *Hurry up, bus.*

Sure enough, a carload of older guys cruises slowly past and they're all staring at us. I'm saying, 'Bro, let's ring Mum to come pick us up.' Johnny's acting all hard, the only way he knows. But he agrees and we head to the petrol station and I use their phone to call Mum. I'm begging, 'Please, Mum, you've got to come get us', just as we see the older guys' car pull up.

They march in and punch Johnny a few times; they must've thought I was too young and skinny to bother with. The staff have just pulled us into the back room when Mum rocks up. She goes off her head at seeing Johnny with a cut above his eye. Good old protective Mum.

Johnny was my other protector. One time at school, a big boy hit me with a cricket bat and Johnny came sprinting over – he was on detention or something – and beats the guy up. Even now when people are saying, 'Oh, Sonny, you made it, you've done real good,' I think of my steadfast brother and inwardly thank him for taking care of me while I developed – and, of course, for warning me not to follow his path when I was fourteen. I truly believe I might not have made it if not for my big brother's love, and I will always be grateful for that. Obviously, we are super close.

Sonny Bill's older brother, John Arthur, would never let anyone hurt his brother. If you wanted a bodyguard, you couldn't get any better than him. He has a sense of humour too.

One day, he and Sonny Bill were leaving a Bulldogs game in separate cars, John Arthur's car in front. This was when Sonny Bill was too shy to say who he was and didn't think he was that good, even though the media and the fans were singing his praises.

John Arthur tells his driver to wait up, gets out and points at Sonny Bill's car. 'Hey! Look who's in that car – it's Sonny Bill!' And as everyone started running over to get a look at Sonny Bill, John Arthur's got back in his car, laughing at the fans mobbing his little bro!

If Sonny Bill was worried about something, John Arthur would bring out his dry sense of humour just to lighten Sonny Bill up. Those two are so close. John Arthur doesn't tell his brother he's played like a star if Sonny Bill's game wasn't quite up to his high standard. He is always straight up with him, which is exactly

what someone like Sonny Bill needs. Praise and compliments
don't make him a better player, constructive criticism does, and
no-one gives it to him straighter – but with total love – than
John Arthur. We're all straight up with him, as family should
be. – Lee Williams

Johnny and I have talked about where his own playing
career might have gone, but he has no regrets along those
lines and only wishes the best for me and our little sister
Niall, also a national representative in two rugby codes.
I'm proud of Niall, but just as proud of my other sister,
Denise, and of Johnny.

I do wonder, too, if Johnny and I might have had an
easier road if Dad had been a better role model. Dad will
admit he was a hard man. I went through a phase where
I did not look up to him, because he was a man of few
words and some of those words could have been kinder.
Once I learned what his childhood was like, I began to
understand him better, but there have been times when
I could have used some paternal wisdom and support.

When I was in my last two years at the Bulldogs, I was
in the headlines for being blind drunk in public or being
with a woman in a bar. I wasn't proud of this, but it
wasn't enough to make me change things. I was caught up
in it all. Johnny was in Australia with me, but because we
were living in that moment we didn't see the immediate

danger. I needed someone to talk things through with me, talk some sense into me, but there wasn't anyone doing that, least of all my old man. And, to be fair, my parents weren't really in a position to help me navigate the world of professional sports, because it was a million miles away from what they knew. I would have to work it out as I went, and at that point I wasn't doing it well.

Sonny Bill was good at phoning or doing FaceTime when he was overseas – not just with me but with all his family. When he first appeared in the newspapers as the eighteen-year-old league star in Sydney, my mum and I would go up the road to buy the papers and then sit down and read every word. It just felt unbelievable, the things they were saying about him being a superstar and all that. We just couldn't believe our boy was all over the newspapers.

After a few years of this, we'd got used to it; we could have built our own library with the amount of stuff written about him. I did take it to heart when negative things were said about him, as any mother would. Then I took the attitude, *They'll say anything to sell newspapers*. One time I read that I was in Australia, when I was sitting here in Auckland with my mum.

You wake up to the media with a son like Sonny Bill. How they use a headline mentioning him just to get your attention, then you read the piece and it's hardly about him at all. They'll use his picture, so naturally you read what they have to say, only to find it's more about someone else, like a teammate who did something silly. To the media, it seems that just playing in the same team is enough to drag you into something.

Of course, if they love you, then you're fine. You're the teacher's pet who can do no wrong, even when everyone knows you are doing wrong. But if they get dirty on someone and start attacking them, they can ruin the person's career, destroy his or her self-confidence.

Does any player like reading harsh criticism about how they played? How would a journalist like it if after every second piece they wrote, their boss wrote a scathing review naming them? But there are good journalists who are fair. I'm just dirty on those who maybe don't think about the consequences for the person they're writing about. Maybe they could take a breath and ask themselves what effect their article will have on the player. – Lee Williams

In later years, I've come to understand I got some of my loving qualities from Dad. He might not have been able to express his love through words, but it was there in his actions. He was always playing cricket with us, and he coached my brother's footy team. Sure, he had a gambling habit, and we all know a gambler loses more than he wins, but if he had money, he'd give it to us. But as a husband? Let's say he was far from Husband of the Year. When one person is drinking and gambling and the other is home looking after four kids, tensions rise. No child ever really knows what goes on between their mother and father. That's just the nature of relationships: sometimes they work, sometimes they don't. You can't change your past, only how you react to it. You can't erase bad memories or bad deeds, or correct poor decisions. You can only learn from them and face the future with a positive mindset.

So, I was a late starter to alcohol, and I might've let it get the better of me a bit, but one thing I can say is I was almost always a lovey-dovey drunk.

* * *

At the start of 2005, I was on seventy grand a year, which to me was a lot of money. I mean a *lot*. I was going to get Mum that house with nice wallpaper, buy Dad a car, look after my brother and twin sisters. Little did I know the player-manager sharks had smelled blood. Dad had moved to Sydney with his new partner, and I just let him choose who would be my manager. Neither of us knew anything about money, so we trusted others to tell us what to do. As it turned out, it wasn't smart to remove ourselves from financial decisions.

I was not making many good decisions at all around that time. One night, I was at this club in Kings Cross drinking with the boys, and these two guys were walking around staring at everyone. It was late and I'd had a few, so I was full of swagger. Thinking I was the man, I deliberately stepped back into one of them.

'Yo, what you doing, bro?!'

He stood his ground. 'Come outside and I'll shoot you in the leg – see how your footy career goes after that.'

I sobered up pretty quickly and had more than second thoughts: I was out of there!

The guy walked off to talk to his mates on the other side of the bar – or maybe to get his gun – and I took my chance and scooted out through the kitchen and hailed a cab. My legs have always been my best asset!

The Doggies would end up barring players from drinking in the Cross. The ban was put in place because of a big fight between a bouncer and one of the boys, but I am sure there were lots of other incidents that no-one ever heard of. Like that one.

This was at a time when I was playing my best footy, and I wasn't able to step back and look at my life. I wasn't mature enough to appreciate the privileged position I was in and see that obligations come with that. People look up to you, kids idolise you, many of them want to become the next Sonny Bill, and I was not taking on the responsibilities that came with that fame.

My natural bent is to overthink things. But I wasn't thinking at all. I wasn't in a good space – or, rather, I felt all that was required of me was to train hard and play hard and, yes, party hard. It's funny; we Islanders often excel physically but ignore the mental side of things. We avoid going a bit deeper and asking ourselves why we behave in certain ways. Yet our Polynesian ancestors were strong and fierce and must have been strong mentally too. Though, admittedly, they did not have a modern lifestyle full of temptations to deal with.

I feel from my own experiences that I'm a good person, but I know now if I'm not held accountable for my actions by something greater than myself, I can lose my way.

Around this time, I knew I was going astray and, like my mum, I wanted to do what was right. I'd met this guy, Khoder Nasser, who was a fight promoter, and I started hanging out with him, intrigued by what he had to say about life in general. He knew everyone and everyone respected him, not only because he was a promoter, but for who he was, his character. It seemed to me they liked him because he was a good man.

Before I started talking to Khoder, I was caught in a spiral of play hard, party hard and I wasn't making good decisions about who I was hanging out with. In a footy club, there are party boys, there are family men, there are guys with good morals and guys with bad morals. And then there are the hangers-on, who are only there for the free booze or drugs and to have a good time. They don't care about you, but you kid yourself they are your mates. I wasn't judging or caring; I was just partying and whoever wanted to join me was the friend I'd spend time with. Thankfully, I came out the other side of this but for a while there it was not good. I've come to realise that to understand someone's character, you can often look at who their five closest friends are. At that time, the people I was hanging with were not known for their good character.

I was looking for something but it took me a while to realise I wouldn't find deeper meaning in a shot glass. I had to walk away from temptations. And that is much harder to do than say. It is something I would struggle with for years, because those temptations are always there.

Khoder had integrity and was a man of his word. When I talked to Khoder about his life, he started telling me a bit about his faith and what being a Muslim meant to him. Gradually, some part of me seized on that. This was something greater than myself.

I was yearning for a deeper meaning to my life. I think a good part of the aching inside was a spiritual need. I'd got through that dark frame of mind when I was first injured, but all this drinking, partying and womanising made me realise I was dressing a deep wound with sticking plaster. I'd always dismissed the wound as low self-esteem, but I was starting to understand that it was more than that. I was heading for a reckoning – with myself.

CHAPTER 3

A curve ball straight to the head

I'm often asked if I had any personal rivalries in league and rugby. I don't think I ever approached a game with the idea of getting the better of any particular individual. I did want to mark out my territory and once on the field, my shyness and low self-esteem ceased to exist. I only wanted to stamp my mark on the game. To be like an animal in the wild, establish my territory. I would want to get the better of any opponent who stood in my way.

It was a massive buzz playing against Gorden Tallis and the Broncos in my first year of NRL and seeing the fearsome man charging at me. No disrespect to Gordie, because we are mates these days, but it was a huge boost for me and the other young Islander boys in the team to see our teammate Roy Asotasi run through him and score a try. It was like announcing a changing of the guard. Us young boys were coming. Tonie Carroll, Shane Webcke and Petero Civoniceva from the Broncos were other players I liked to go up against. It was never overwhelming for me; it was more like excitement mixed with adrenaline. Same when I went to play rugby: I loved playing against the biggest names.

Playing against other Islanders or Kiwis was also a big buzz because we play a physical style of game. We're all big and brutal and can do the physicality thing all day long. I remember playing for the New Zealand Test side after only a few NRL games for the Bulldogs. Man, playing for my country at only eighteen – against Australia, the best team in the world – was a big moment.

I came on in the forwards and ended up playing some big minutes. I remember being very physical with every man headed my way. I loved it! That was my mentality back then: I was the young guy trying to prove himself, to show that I belonged out there, playing with and against the big boys. I'd attempt to smash the biggest or strongest guy on the field, even though I was still in a boy's body. Unfortunately, we lost that game to Australia 37–10.

At the end of that year, I'd be named in the New Zealand team for the Tri-Nations Test and would line up against Australia in Auckland. Being on the big stage back in my home town was a thrill and I managed to carry on my form from the Dogs season and won the Man of the

Match award in front of my family and friends. It was a huge accomplishment for a nineteen-year-old.

I was playing for New Zealand, playing for the Bulldogs and it was all happening. I didn't care who I was going up against. I was there to play. But I did love playing against the Polynesian/Māori-stacked Warriors. We all try to give back what we receive!

As a youngster, before I left New Zealand, a few of us in the New Zealand under-16s team were invited to train with the Warriors and their development team. In that team, there was one particular player who went on to carve out a magnificent career (I am not going to name him). My best mate's older brother grew up with him. They had been friends since they were kids. We're in the gym on the bikes, and this guy walks in and I'm like, 'Hey, bro!', then calling him by his first name. I was excited at seeing someone from my hood. I said my best mate's older brother's name and told him he said to say hello.

This guy gets on the bike beside me, looks me up and down, and doesn't say a word. Just turns away and starts biking. I was so embarrassed. Some years later, he and I were playing in the same team and I never said a word to him about the incident, though I never forgot that snub. It gave me the motivation to play my best footy whenever we met the Warriors. And to always respect and give the young boys coming through my time.

A couple of years later, in my next encounter with the Warriors, Stacey Jones was still playing for them and the game was a big deal. I got forty or fifty tickets for my family and friends. Their old guys were typical Kiwi boys out to put shots on you. Fine. Bring it. This was my element.

I remember Clinton Toopi targeted me early on. To be honest, I was a little flattered that he knew who I was. But this type of thing on the footy field didn't phase me at all. I was actually quite used to it. It took me back to the games I used to play against South Auckland footy teams like Māngere East or Ōtāhuhu, playing against massive Islanders putting it on you. And to survive, I had to give them a taste of a fierce shoulder charge.

In this game, Clinton ran the ball from dummy half and in I went with the biggest shoulder charge – bang! Down he went. I also tackled Stacey Jones and ripped the ball off him. I remember thinking, *I've just done that to none other than Stacey Jones.*

During that game, I managed to make a break from inside our half and then put our fullback under the posts for a try. Doing all this in front of my friends and family in New Zealand was something I will never forget.

Later that year, we played the Panthers in the first preliminary final at the Sydney Football Stadium. They had a massive pack like us, led by two of the best Islander players at the time – Tony Puletua and Joe Galuvao. They were called the 'hair bears'. Man, they were playing some exciting footy. In that same game, Steve Price, our captain, went down injured. Coach Steve Folkes called me over and said, 'I'm going to need you to play prop. Are you up for it?' I said sweet, even though on the inside I had moments of fear, most of all of letting my teammates down.

But I kept it simple, a formula I'd bank on for years to come. Stay in the game, work hard, do all the little things my teammates respect and the magic will come. Follow a good deed with a good deed and a bad one with a good one. Thankfully, I ended up playing well and we won. We were off to the grand final.

In the 2004 final against the Sydney Roosters, their feared English enforcer, Adrian Morley, put a hit on me. I just thought, *That wasn't so bad. Is that all you got?* Like Ali said to George Foreman in their Rumble in the Jungle in Zaire in 1974: 'That all you got, George? I thought you hit harder than that!' It was the biggest upset win in heavyweight boxing history – and at the end of that grand final thirty years later, we upset a fair few when we held up the premiership trophy.

In that grand final, as soon as I entered the field I put a massive shoulder charge on, and the crowd went crazy. I knew I was ready for the biggest game of my young career. To be honest, it was nothing new to my 2004 'Dogs of War' teammates. Hits like that is what we did to each other at training, with hardened players like Mark O'Meley, Willie Mason, Reni Maitua, Hutch Maiava, Roy Asotasi, Adam Perry and Steve Price flying into each other and me. Our whole Dogs team did it and that was only practice. We took that into game day and we were ahead of the pack from practising for real. We had the flash in the backs of Willie Tonga, Johnathan Thurston, Matt Utai, Hazem El Masri, Braith Anasta and Brent Sherwin. Our forward pack was big and ruthless. I mean *ruthless*.

But I fitted that mould, and the coach and guys I was playing with had helped me become that ruthless player. I'm proud that in those last two games of the 2004 season I showed I could do the tough stuff as well as the flash stuff. At the end of that game, we were crowned the NRL champions of 2004.

But here's the thing: if I've played well, I feel like I'm part of the team and I deserve to be there. If I had a bad game, it's the opposite: I feel so down on myself, like I don't belong and only ever will as long as I keep having good games.

That's how a lot of the players feel, as if the game and only the game defines who and what they are. That's why lots of us fall apart when we retire, turn into boozers, get hooked on drugs, become the pub bore living in the past and often die way too young from poor health issues. Falling from the top of sport to forgotten, and becoming a shadow of your former magnificent physical self on the way down, has to be so hard to accept. I was starting to understand how complicated a player's life can become when either the physical or mental starts to suffer. I distinctly remember straight after that 2004 grand final being overwhelmed by an intense joy. It fuelled the celebrations. But then, a few days later, that was gone and I was left with an aching feeling of emptiness. The thought, *Is that it?* went through my mind. I know now how important it is to have gratitude for everything that happens to you and to always reset and give yourself a new dream to chase.

A contact sports career doesn't usually last longer than ten to twelve years, and many players are only at their peak for six or seven years and then are dropped, never to be heard of again. Luckily, my career extended many years beyond that, and the fact that I got to play four different sports – if boxing can be called 'play'! – is a privilege I appreciate more as I get older. But I have also learned that I need more than sport in my life to feel right and live well. I have carried a knee injury since I was twenty. At the time, a surgeon told me I might have only two years left of playing. No way was I accepting that. I deliberately targeted that knee area in training by building strength around it. I feel for players whose careers suddenly end at, say, age twenty-seven or twenty-eight. To go from big star to forgotten is a long way to plummet. And some of the fans demand so much of their heroes, yet as soon as they drop in form, it's out of sight, out of mind.

Even after that incredible year of my first premier season, things started to feel out of whack because all I was focused on was sport. I knew where I stood when I was playing, but the party hard after-game culture was starting to throw me off balance. And throughout most of that year, the whole team had had to deal with a harsh media spotlight after rape allegations were made against unnamed players after a pre-season trial match. The lead detective later came out and said the allegations didn't stack up, but every member of the team had to visit police headquarters in Sydney for questioning and to submit a DNA sample. I was a young bloke with my family in New Zealand, so I didn't have much to say, but others in the team spoke out about how that impacted them and their families. Everywhere the team went, there were cameras on us. Our every facial expression was discussed and even what we wore was commented on. Each one of us was under suspicion until the police declared that no player would be charged and there was no evidence to pursue. That was my first experience of how something can be amplified before the evidence is examined, and how judgements can be made by the media and the public without anyone knowing the full story.

That's the thing with elite sport. There are many, many benefits that come your way, but there are things that can be difficult to handle, especially if you are a young bloke living away from family and friends and suddenly in a bubble that removes you in some ways from everyday life. You have to work hard not to lose touch with your own moral compass.

And I get it: with fame comes expectations, especially in the sporting world. I think being a boy with such low self-esteem didn't help me either. I never felt like I belonged with all those big stars. So the idea that I was not only a star, but a role model, was hard to come to terms with. It made me feel unsettled and unsure of myself. Nowadays, being a role model is something I am proud to be and take very seriously.

* * *

Let's fast-forward to 2012. I was coming off a successful 2011 World Cup campaign and also a Crusaders Super Rugby season and I was starting to feel at ease in the fifteen-man game. To be closer to Mum, I signed with the Hamilton-based Chiefs. I still felt like I had a lot to prove as a union man and joining a club that wasn't considered a title contender was the best place to do it. And what a season it turned out to be!

Unknown to me and my new teammates at the time, that year would see the start of a fierce rivalry between my old club and my new one. Although there was no expectation on us from fans, media and the like – we were labelled one of the least likely teams to win the 2012 Super Rugby title – that didn't stop our squad from working hard during the off-season to be ready for the ambush we intended to unleash on the rest of the Super Rugby franchises.

After twelve weeks of boxing preparation, which resulted in me winning the New Zealand Professional Boxing Association (NZPBA) Heavyweight Championship belt, I came into the pre-season team training a lot later than most of the others. I was mentally fresh and in the best physical shape I'd ever been in, but I was quickly made aware that so too were my teammates. That mentality of striving to get better as an athlete but also now as a Chiefs' team member was expected not just of me but all of us.

Like me, Dave Rennie was also in his first year at the club. He may have been the captain of the ship, but below the deck Liam Messam was also laying the foundations for us to thrive as a team. We had started pretty well in the competition but I'd say most people didn't take us seriously until we went up against my old teammates at the Crusaders. From that game's first whistle, the battle began and a fierce rivalry ignited that is still alight today.

There was lots of niggle between All Blacks teammates, and lots of lead changes saw a tough, uncompromising game end with a Chiefs' 24–19 victory. Performances like that don't just happen overnight, a lot of hard work and prep go into them. As a team, we still had many mountains to climb, but it was a great feeling beating the competition favourite and starting to see the fruits of our labour. We had just put everyone on notice that the Chiefs of 2012 were no longer the easybeats of the competition.

Questions were still being asked about us by some: 'Can they keep this form up?', 'Can they deal with the expectation of fans?', 'Can they sustain this effort for the whole season?' and 'Do they have what it takes?'

The answer to them all was an emphatic, 'YES!'

Our season, off the back of hard mahi (work) on the field and great camaraderie driven by everyone loving being in each other's company off field, had me feeling completely at ease. Crudz, Liam, and many other of my Chiefs teammates and I were having world-class seasons to remember as players and it was all focused on one goal. A goal we were edging closer to. Deep down, though we never spoke about it, we all knew which team we'd have to beat if our franchise was to win our first-ever championship: the Crusaders. Even though we'd beaten them in the early stages of the season, that hadn't stopped many people believing they would win the comp. With over 90 per cent of their starting team having played for the All Blacks, it would have been hard not to think they would finish at the top of the ladder. But we put paid to that when we topped the leader board at the end of the regular round and earned ourselves a home semi-final against them.

I've played in World Cup finals and big pressure games, but there's something about playing against some of your good mates in a huge contest that makes it that much more special. Maybe it is the pride of not wanting someone you know so well to get one over you, or maybe it is wanting to make your close ones proud on home soil – like I used to try to do all those years ago by putting on massive shoulder charges to get the praise of my big brother. Either way, my teammates rose to the challenge. This game is one of my favourite games of my sporting career across all codes.

We won the game 20–17. Against my former teammates and a Crusaders' side stacked with current All Blacks, we all had a night to remember. I had a hand in the first three tries and was a physical presence everywhere on the field.

In the first lineout of the game, my man Benny Tameifuna pushed their captain and leader out of the way. It was a very unexpected play, and some say it is the memory of that, and other actions that night, that still keeps the flames of that fierce rivalry going. I know that act had me thinking that reputation meant nothing out there that night. It was our time.

The next week, we played the Sharks in the final and we won 37–6. I scored a late try and then jumped into the crowd as a sign of my appreciation to the Chiefs' faithful. We were the Super Rugby 2012 Champions. I still get goosebumps remembering that night. Who would have thought?

* * *

Of course, it's not just the rivalries that inspire you to lift your game. It's the guys in your own team who you want to excel for. When I played with Aaron Cruden in the 2012 Chiefs team, we developed an almost spiritual connection, like we could read each other, feel one another's presence. I think we were two players with something to prove and that connection shone bright in every game.

I think our playing styles complemented each other really well. We were both keen and eager to improve and grow as players.

We would talk about different situations that might occur on
the field and what we needed to do to create a positive outcome
for the team. Sometimes you just have automatic synergy with
another player and that was the case between Sonny and me.
He certainly made my job easier and enjoyable with his X-factor
play-making ability. Sonny's work ethic was always top shelf and
it became infectious for others around him. I remember a contact
training we had, the boys were ripping into each other, as they do.
Then Sonny stepped forward to put one of his trademark big hits
on Ben Tameifuna, who weighed a healthy 135 kilograms. The
collision was brutal with both players giving 110 per cent, neither
player backed down from the challenge. The rest of the team just
stopped, looked at each other and there was a collective feeling
that we all needed to bring more intensity into our sessions if
we wanted to be successful. That moment really set the tone
and the standard for the rest of the season. These types of
moments happened regularly around Sonny. He was someone who
was completely dedicated to his craft, he was never satisfied
and always pushed boundaries. This mindset contributed to
his greatness. And it was a pleasure to get the chance to play
alongside him. — Aaron Cruden

When the Chiefs' opportunity came up for me, they were
ranked thirteenth out of fifteen Super teams, but that
didn't bother me. In fact, I relished the challenge. When
Dave Rennie asked if I wanted to come on board, I was in.

It was one of the best decisions I ever made. I am forever grateful to the franchise and to the people of Hamilton who helped me fall in love with the game of rugby.

I had a lot to prove. I wanted to show that I was one of the best players in my position and I deserved to be there at the highest level. That goal lit a ferocious fire in me and I was driven to show what I could do.

Liam Messam was there, and we became like brothers, really close. My cousin Tim Nanai-Williams, Aaron Cruden, Liam and I all had something to prove. People were saying we were a team of supposed deadbeats who'd lost too many games. They were wrong. What I found when I signed with the Chiefs was a bunch of guys totally committed to each other and determined to turn things around. We were all burning with that desire.

Aaron and I played together in every game and it gave us a deep understanding of each other's styles. Liam and my cousin were in the same zone. It seemed like we'd been playing together our whole careers. The special plays we were all coming up with out on the field were a reflection of how tight we all were and the natural flair we had. The future stars in our team of nobodies – guys like Brodie Retallick, Robbie Robinson at fullback, Lelia Masaga on the wing, hooker Hika Elliot, Sam Cane, Tim Nanai-Williams, Augustine Pulu, Tawera Kerr-Barlow, Richard Kahui, Tanerau Latimer and Ben Tameifuna – were ready.

Everyone in that team had an awesome connection. It didn't matter what colour you were, or where you were from, everyone's feet were firmly on the ground.

Our careers kind of went hand-in-hand, playing together in the Chiefs, in international Tests. We had the same spots on the team bus. I remember one time on the bus, Sonny asked to hotspot my phone. I asked how come he had no data.

'I forget to pay my phone bills, bro.' He then admitted his power got cut off quite often because he forgot to pay his power bill.

The buzz in the team at hearing he was joining the Chiefs was unreal. His performances in 2012 were outstanding. He got Player of the Year. Absolutely deserved because of his influence on all of us, but especially as a role model for the Polynesian players. He lifted their level of professionalism and we all took inspiration from his incredible training routine.

I remember one end of year with the All Blacks, we finished up in Cardiff. Sonny had this cool necklace, which he offered to me to wear that night. Luckily, I put it in my room.

In the morning, everyone woke with sore heads, and we went out to the bus taking us to the airport. Sonny asked for his necklace. I couldn't remember where I'd left it. He said it cost him five grand! I was near pooping myself, scrambling through my gear bag looking for it, thinking I'd have to pay him $5000. Thank God I'd thrown it in my bag.

Over the years of playing in the All Blacks together, he opened up with those of us close to him. We still tracked each other for the number of Tests we played. We'd have chats about different Tests and Dane Coles and I were league fans, so we'd drill him about different games and players.

We knew from his time in the Chiefs he was big on family. He shared his vulnerabilities with us, which we appreciated. As rugby players, we are supposed to be tough dudes with no vulnerabilities. Give me the vulnerable Sonny Bill. The honest man, the good man. – Sam Cane

Sammy is a man I'd follow into battle any day. When I was out there on the field, I'd love looking up and seeing Sam next to me. I'd know it was time to go hunting.

Dave Rennie, of Rarotongan extraction, was a shrewd coach with the kind of street skills that had him change tactics depending on who we played. He took away the opposition's strengths and played to ours. He allowed us to play a freer game and helped us hit the opposition with surprises. That's where the offloads really came to the fore. And as much as I admire Dave, he would be the first to agree that a team needs talented, quality players with a determined attitude and a total team commitment to win consistently. Players who refuse to be dominated by, let alone lie down for, an opposition with a far bigger forward pack, a swifter backline. The Chiefs were a team that fitted perfectly with my work ethic and, man, they sure worked hard at every moment of every practice, and anyone who slackened off found someone eager to take his place.

We were all expressing ourselves on the field and my offloads became the norm and what most of the team did. We connected on the field and that was reflected off the field as well. On trips away, the likes of Hika Elliot on guitar had us all expressing ourselves with our singing voices. Though Hika sang enough for everyone! I know I've talked before about us Polynesians and Māori being naturally shy around others. I think that comes from growing up in a culture that demands strict respect for older people. But we can change that and pull the personality out of each other when we get together because we know each of us is vulnerable, a bit socially hesitant, just with that bro-talk, the laughter, the classic eyebrow-lift in greeting, the 'You all right, bro?', the 'Chur, bro', the knowing looks followed by a giggle, a sly mirrored grin. There were plenty of funny characters in that team to get us laughing, and we were always in stitches at funny jokes or word plays – but only off the field. On the field, it was pure focus and a passion to win. Those guys, that team, created the perfect environment to bring out the best in me, on the field and off.

It was the Chiefs' first championship win in the seventeen-year history of the competition. I think the ESPN report on the game says it all: 'The Chiefs won this game not because of one big-name match-winner, but because they have forged an unrivalled team spirit – they would not be beaten.'

Some people get caught up in that world of, 'What's in it for me?' But the age-old adage that in giving you receive is what it is all about, as I was coming to understand. It's not about wanting, wanting, wanting everything for me, myself and I. Rather, it's about giving of your whole self to another, giving your time, your aroha, your sympathetic ear. That's what it means to be not just a great sportsman, but a decent human being. I feel like at the Chiefs we all learned that it isn't about star players, it is about playing as a team and *for* the team, watching out for each other and leaving it all on the field, because that is what teamwork means.

* * *

Being a decent human being and talking about the choices that lead you there is way more important to me than talking about my offloads, but I do know rugby and league heads want to know every detail about them. And I obviously enjoy doing them!

When I first came to All Blacks rugby in 2010, I brought my offloads with me, but I soon picked up the coaches' attitude to them: *It's not how we play rugby.*

I think the action was a bit before its time in 2010. But I'd faced the same attitude in rugby league in my earlier days. The coaches couldn't get their minds around it, despite the obvious advantages. I didn't understand why they couldn't see this. In the 2011 World Cup semi-final against Australia, I remember assistant coach Steve Hansen saying, 'Whatever you do, don't offload.'

Fast-forward to the 2015 Rugby World Cup and it was a different story. The same man would agree that one of the biggest weapons in my arsenal was my second-play-creating offload. It even had a name: 'KBA' – keeping the ball alive. I offloaded in the final on the biggest stage with my first two touches of the ball. It resulted in Ma'a Nonu scoring to give us a handy lead. I think now if I hadn't backed myself and pushed the boundaries, would I still have achieved what I did? Would I still have played with the All Blacks?

In my younger days playing rugby league, I'd had a coach sub me off for offloading. Another time, I was pulled off the field for picking up the ball with one hand and spilling it.

The thing about the offload is it's such a vital part of the game, especially when done correctly. With that glass-half-full on-field mentality coming naturally, I've always been one to test the boundaries and go for the offload when no-one expects it. Big plays in big matches change the course of the game.

I love seeing young guys playing without fear and just expressing themselves, doing things coaches can't coach, just like they would have done as youngsters out in the backyard. I think that's the difference between New Zealand teams and the teams in a lot of other countries. Nowadays in New Zealand, you are taught to back yourself on the field because that's when the magic happens. Another example of this is the Fiji rugby sevens: they are so hard to defend against because you don't know what will happen next. They are the Harlem Globetrotters of sevens rugby and it resulted in them winning the first ever Olympic gold medal for their country. What a special sight that was! And they backed that up in Tokyo in 2021 with another gold medal.

In the 2013 NRL grand final, if I hadn't stayed on the opposite side of the field from where I was supposed to be to attack a gap I'd seen, I wouldn't have got that short ball off Sam Moa and put a flying James Maloney away to take the lead in the biggest game of the year.

In the 2015 Rugby World Cup Final against Australia, I went out and made a statement with two offloads. Out on the biggest stage, I shook off my off-field insecurities and backed myself with the mentality: *You gotta play, Sonny. Play. Be in the game. When you get the ball, you know what to do with it.* Out there, I backed myself, I trusted my skills and preparation, and I did what I always do: followed my instincts.

If players don't trust their instincts and push the boundaries, there is no growth. Sure, we need to stick to the majority of the game plan, but the game plan needs to have the space built in so that players can express themselves and have the freedom to find the magic. Polynesians and Māoris have a lot of that natural flair and if it wasn't for coaches like Todd Blackadder, Steve Folkes and Dave Rennie pushing me to express myself on the field, who knows, I might not have overcome my lack of confidence off the field and allowed that and my inner critic to affect the way I played. I may not have trusted myself enough to fully step into that space and I may never have reached my full potential and stood up in those big games. When you do and it is all going right, nothing feels better.

Those are the good times. But sometimes it's a double-edged sword. The red card in the Lions series, for example. I truly believed I was going to give my brothers a psychological advantage, smoke the guy, demonstrate physical dominance having come off a personally very good performance in the first Test. I told myself:

Be aggressive, Sonny. Be physical. What happens? The guy ducks and my shoulder slams into his head. I am making history as only the second All Black to receive a red card. At the time, I felt so ashamed for letting down not just my team but my country.

Looking back on it now, I know I was just doing my best. The truth is, you can't win 'em all. There are going to be times when you get clipped in the boxing ring, spill a ball, drop a pass. But the *I'm not good enough* Islander mentality could really weigh me down sometimes, and no amount of media praise for the vast majority of my playing career could change it. I've had some incredible press and I might have this big name, I've heard Keven Mealamu and Jerome Kaino – two of the All Blacks greats – complimenting me, but I don't hold on to any of that. I have struggles like everyone else. The struggle doesn't stop, and even when you think you've got life sussed, got it all figured out, there's that curve ball coming straight for your head.

CHAPTER 4

You can't run from the man in the mirror

Injuries are part of an athlete's life. We all carry them, and you just have to hope that with good luck and good management they won't end your career too early, before you've had a chance to prove what you can do. I've seen some heartbreaking injuries stop great players in their tracks. I've got a list of dodgy body parts. At the top of that list is the curve ball I've known about for some time: my crook knee. I must have had close to fifteen knee operations on the same knee; I've got no cartilage there now, which pretty much means it is bone on bone. It is crazy to think I have stayed a sportsman for so long. Maybe without the knee issue, I could have gone on another two years, because of my training and the drive I've always had. My knee was a daily struggle that

I just had to fit into my routine, the daily maintenance of recovering.

But let me rewind back to the start. My first big operation was when I was seventeen and had a major ligament reattached in my shoulder. Once I was back playing, I forgot all about it. But my knee injury was so severe they took out all the cartilage on my meniscus, and I had bone bruising and a bit of bone chipped off.

The doctor at the Dogs at the time – he's now passed away – was a good fella by the name of Hugh Hazard. He was this old Aussie dude who was always smoking. He told me I had to be careful, or within a couple of years I wouldn't be able to play anymore. I heard this and thought, *Really? My career could be over by twenty-three?*

That situation shaped a lot of my life for the next fourteen years. I spent so much time taking care of my knee: rehab, stretching, building the muscle around it, going to the pool, using an ice machine not just after a game but after every training session. Sometimes nothing could stop it swelling up but that just steeled me, prepared me better for going hard in the latter years. That good doctor had planted a seed in my head, and I was determined that I'd be around longer than two years. I'd last another five years at least. That's the number I carried around in my head. *Five years. Five years, Sonny.*

Injuries dogged my career, like they do a lot of sportspeople. I suffered a slipped disc in my back. Did my Achilles in the first game of the Olympics rugby sevens. But, then, I reckon a lot of good came from this knee, because it changed my mental attitude to sport. It was never just a matter of training and playing hard, but preparing as well as I possibly could and doing all those little one-percenters that might not sound much but which, added up, can make the difference between winning and losing. I used an ice machine for a good ten years and I don't think any opposition knew about the knee or they would have targeted it, big time.

I was taking painkillers and anti-inflammatories almost daily and always before a game in the last five years of playing just to get on the field. There's this product you can inject into the knee that acts like a buffer, but that's not enough; if I don't keep up my rehab routine it starts to really ache, because I've got mad arthritis. That's why boxing is such a good sport for me: less stressful on the joints, the knees, it's more about upper body effort and moving.

And it's not just my knee that is dodgy. One thing about the shoulder charge: if you get the timing slightly wrong, you'll come off second best. My left shoulder has given me quite a lot of grief over the years. That carries over to boxing and throwing a left hook, most orthodox boxers' favourite shot. Think David Tua. I have to adjust to get the little left shoulder muscles firing so I can throw the shot.

My body carries the memories of every game and every fight. But I was taught how to look after my body. The teams had doctors and physios and whoever or whatever else you needed to help get your body right. I may not have valued school enough to pay attention, but I was attentive and diligent to everything I was taught in regards to my knee. But it was my mind that really got messed up in the early years. And there was nobody watching out for that, or showing me how to fix things.

In 2004, I was on top of the world. I had more than any young man could wish for, especially one coming from my background. Right? Wrong. I was just a young man trying to come to grips with who I was, what I wanted to be and how to achieve it.

But where was the book on that? Who did I go to? I didn't have any authority figure or role model to talk with, to ask for guidance. There was no-one to steer me onto the right path. You see, in sport, if you excel at it, everyone considers you The Man. You can do no wrong, even when it's obvious you are doing just that. I'm not saying I was ever a bad person; I never lost the manners taught to me by Mum and by Nan, and it is in my nature to be polite. I was still shy, hardly said boo to anyone off the field. But I was a slave to my lusts and desires. I made bad choices and didn't do myself or my family proud.

The fact is, I was struggling with who I was on the inside. On one hand, I was this supposed star, this big-time sportsman who had it all. Yet inside I had nothing. That's what I went through in stage one of my rugby league career, aged eighteen to twenty-one.

The plaster kept getting put over the wound, but, as I discovered, you can't hide from yourself. Injuries and alcohol fuelled some bad behaviour and I made mistakes. I am not going to justify them. They were my doing. But having my mum see the headlines when I was caught peeing in an alleyway was not great. And that was the tip of the iceberg.

In those years, I had my share of women; some might say I was promiscuous. But I was a young guy and that's what all the guys around me were doing. I was just following the group, not questioning whether it was right or wrong. What young man turns down a beautiful woman? The society I moved in condoned and even lauded that behaviour. I actually had my own internal moral code, which is why I always felt really bad whenever I ditched a woman and moved on to the next. Inside, I knew it was wrong, and when you're a shy, polite person like I've always been, that inner turmoil is a wild storm. But feeling bad is not the same as knowing how to do something about it.

That wasn't the full extent of my bad choices. There is no excuse for the drink-driving, for which I deserved the media avalanche. I had stayed at a friend's place after a night out and was headed home early the next morning, not thinking for a moment I was over the limit. But I was on my P plates and so I shouldn't have had any alcohol in my system at all. In hindsight, I can see our Bulldogs CEO was managing a situation, but in doing that he ignored what was happening to me. If he really cared about my wellbeing, he wouldn't have put me in front of a hungry media pack while I was in such a vulnerable state. Yes, I had been binge drinking, but it was symptomatic of a greater battle that needed to be confronted, and I wasn't strong enough or confident enough to do that on my own. I didn't have the words to tell people that I was feeling overwhelmed or depressed, and no-one saw my behaviour as a red flag or something to ask about. There was no conversation from anyone about my wellbeing at all. I was told to admit publicly I had a drinking problem and sent on a course for problem drinkers. The drinking was a symptom of a much bigger issue that was never once addressed and nobody paid any attention to that. I did need help, but a short course like the one I was signed up for wasn't the medicine I needed for the deep wound I was carrying.

I'm not making excuses; I'm ashamed of the things I did back then and they clash with who I know I am. It might sound strange, but I can't say I'd change anything if I could because without all the things that I went through I might not have had the knowledge and personal insight to have found the biggest blessing of my life – Islam. As brother Malcolm X said: 'Only from the depths of darkness can one reach the greatest of lights.' So, despite my shame, I had to hit my personal rock bottom to finally confront the man I saw when I looked in the mirror.

There were other moments when, caught up in the party-hard culture after a game, I drank too much, took drugs and let myself down. And then there was an incident in a nightclub in 2007, when I fooled around with a woman in a toilet stall. Both she and I will have to live with that mistake for the rest of our lives. It made headlines around a good part of the world. It was embarrassing, and not just for myself. There's the woman involved, of course, though she was a single adult woman and so it really was no-one else's business what she did. But I had a girlfriend at home who was publicly humiliated as well as suffering the pain of being cheated on. She surely did not deserve to be at the centre of a media storm.

I understood the reason I was struggling. The party culture, the money, the access to drugs and alcohol. I was wrestling with it but I wasn't saying no. I was selfish and I had no-one to answer to. Like so many young people in today's society, I had no boundaries and I was struggling to put some up on my own. It was up to me, but I didn't know what to do about it or how to do that. Gradually, it became clear to me I had to change everything. Once I became a committed Muslim and adopted a totally different lifestyle, the fog started to clear. But believe me, it took quite a while for conversion to happen, for me to reject what felt like an enjoyable lifestyle as a party boy. All humans are resistant to changing their ways. And temptations are always there so it is easy to slip back.

This was part of the change that saw me leave the Bulldogs. I was starting to learn more about Islam and the Muslim faith, and my friendships with people like Anthony Mundine and Khoder Nasser were being noticed and commented on. I turned up to training one day and the coach said to me, 'You aren't turning Muslim, are you?'

I tried to laugh it off, but then comments were made about my friends, and that made me very uncomfortable and angry. No-one had paid attention to my private life before then; no-one cared when I was drinking or partying hard as long as I was doing what they needed on the field and it didn't make the press. And even then, it was all about damage control, not about my wellbeing. Yet now, when I was trying to get myself right, suddenly my private life was a concern because of religion.

It all came to a head in 2008. I thought, *I've got to get out of here. Make a complete break, start afresh*

YOU CAN'T RUN FROM THE MAN IN THE MIRROR

somewhere else. I asked Khoder, who had taken over as my manager by then, to look into the possibility of a contract with a Super League club.

That was when Tana Umaga, the first Sāmoan to captain the All Blacks, called me out of the blue from Toulon in the South of France. 'Would you like to consider changing codes to rugby union and play with the team I'm coaching here?' he asked.

A Sāmoan superstar wanted me to switch codes and play in a foreign country just as I'm heading into a personal crisis and wanting out from the Bulldogs, out from Australia, and an opportunity just to reset everything?

I was wrestling with it all but I couldn't see how I could stay. I was scared what would happen. As I said, people were starting to talk about the fact that I was keeping company with Muslims, asking why I was hanging out with 'those kind of people' – 'those' as in Muslims. This just brought out the steel in me and raised my hackles. Like my mum, I will not be told who I can mix with, not by anyone. Choosing my company is my right, as it is yours. If only I could have understood earlier that I needed to change for my own happiness, contentment and to find inner peace rather than blotting out all that need in the noise of partying. I was well aware my sudden departure from the Bulldogs would not go down well

101

with my teammates and fans. I don't blame them for being angry. Or for the wider community declaring they hated me. But no-one knew what was going through my mind and why I felt I had no alternative but to run away.

At the time, though, I could hardly make a press statement explaining the dark place I was in and how I could see no way out. I was overwhelmed but didn't even understand myself why I had lost my way so badly, so had no idea how to explain it to the media, the faithful Bulldogs fans, the coaches and team support staff. If I had known how, maybe things would have been different, but I wasn't able to open up like that. It wasn't something I was doing lightly; I wrestled with it and knew I wasn't just disrupting my own life – it was going to impact my teammates, my family and what people thought of me, something that I had always cared a great deal about. Normally I was so worried about doing the wrong thing or upsetting people that I did nothing and bottled up my feelings. Finally I understood the problem was me and I had to do something to heal myself.

Once I'd decided I would take up Tana Umaga's offer, he said I needed a Sāmoan passport, as apparently there would be fewer visa problems than if I was travelling on my New Zealand passport. So, off to Sāmoa we went, Khoder and myself. I'd been in touch with one of my cousins and we went to his village. They gave me a big welcome, and someone knew someone who knew – you know how it goes.

Tuila'epa Sa'ilele Malielegaoi, the Prime Minister of Sāmoa? Yep. Second day in Apia and there I am sitting having a cup of tea with the PM. He said, 'Are you going to play for Sāmoa? Because if you are, I can get you the passport right now.' I managed a few words in Sāmoan. He called on his driver, who took me down to the passport office, where they were expecting me and knew who had sent me. *No problem, Sonny Bill.* Someone even asked if I wanted a bus driver's licence too! With the passport all sorted, I returned to Sydney. Khoder was promoting Anthony Mundine's next fight, which was to take place in five days' time, so he arranged for his brother, Ahmed, who we call Honks, to travel with me to France via Singapore and London. I'd thrown my phone away, but even before we left, Honks' phone started going off. 'The news is out, bro!' Someone had called a radio station to say they'd seen me at the airport. It was like some weird action movie . . . almost!

At immigration, the guy at the counter calls me over and asks gruffly, 'Where are you going?'

'France.'

'Why are you going there?'

'Um, for a holiday.'

I am a bad liar and didn't sound convincing.

I couldn't wait to get on the plane. When we finally boarded, it felt like an eternity before the doors closed. I was praying that we would take off before the police could board and drag me off the plane. I was so relieved when we were finally airborne, but then I just had my thoughts to worry about.

When we landed in Singapore, Khoder called and told Honks that the Bulldogs administration were trying to subpoena me for breach of contract. I found out later I was the only player in Australian rugby league history to have his club take such action against him. The NRL was also looking to take legal action. The media were waiting for me at Changi Airport with a heap of questions.

Finally, we were on the plane again, but our troubles still weren't over. Going through immigration at London's Heathrow, the guy at the counter looked at my passport and asked, 'What is this?'

'A Sāmoan passport, sir.'

I had to get a map and show him where Sāmoa was.

He told me, 'You can't enter France with this passport. You can enter Britain only.'

I had no clue why this would be the case, but I wasn't up for arguing. I spent two days hiding out in London while the passport problem was sorted. The media were trying to find me, the guy with the subpoena was supposedly looking for me. The manager we signed the contract with was Tana's guy, so we stayed with him, holed up in the attic of a house in Wimbledon, not daring to go out. I spent a lot of time thinking, not really talking to anyone. Every morning I was there, I woke up with a migraine and the thought kept going through my head, *Did I do the right thing?* I was so grateful Honks was with me. He knew the magnitude of the situation and he also knew how to lighten the mood. I love my brother Honks. Finally, we were told I had to go to a consulate somewhere near Hyde Park to get a visa. Honks gets a car, drives me to the visa office and I run in while he parks nearby. I got things sorted and then sprinted out with my visa, convinced I was moments away from being arrested and sent to jail – for breaching a footy contract! That's how naive I was back then.

To avoid the media certain to be waiting for me at Toulon, we flew to Biarritz on the western coast of France. There, I went to a local gym in Pau to work out, and someone recognised me. So I rushed back to the hotel, where the manager – a Frenchman – told me and Honks to pack our things because the media were on to us. This was at about 6 pm. They put me in the car boot and covered me with blankets. Talk about living like a fugitive in a spy drama.

Honks and I drove about eight hours to Tana's house, where I found out that because of legal problems with the contract, I couldn't start playing straight away. The NRL hired lawyers in France, that's how badly they wanted me back. Then I ended up having a big blow-up with Khoder because, back in Australia, Labor powerbroker Graham Richardson had negotiated a settlement down from the asking price of $1.5 million to $750,000 plus $200,000 legal fees and another €70,000 for the French lawyers. Lawyer Mark O'Brien was helping me with the details. I didn't have that kind of money, so Anthony Mundine and some close friends paid it between them. I will never forget their generosity. Half a million each is big bucks to throw at a mate. Now I was in debt big time, and I still didn't know if I was definitely going to be able to play.

But, on the bright side, I was now free to reinvent myself. It was time to address the problems I had and have a long hard discussion with that man in the mirror. I didn't know what would happen. All I knew at that moment was things had to change.

CHAPTER 5

Finding a good space

The perception that I walked out on the Doggies, in breach of my contract, just for money and to try out another rugby code isn't the true story. There are grains of truth in that version, but not the whole salt mine. After I left, I was horrified to be told that, according to *Zoo Weekly*, I was the most hated person in Australia, placed ahead of the Bali Bomber. But just like you can't stop the sun from shining, life goes on and so has mine. I had a lot of turmoil still to go through but years later, after I retired, some really humbling words were said about me. I guess it shows how I conducted myself on and off the field made a positive impact on some people.

Sonny would be the best athlete I've coached from a pure athlete sense . . . As he has got older, he has matured. His training habits and his off-field habits are world class now. He will be a good role model for the young fellas in the club. – Steve Hansen

He's been a great role model for both codes. Especially for young kids growing up in New Zealand, who don't feel like they get the opportunities everyone else gets. What he's shown is that with hard work and determination, you can do whatever you want. You've got to give him full credit, not only for what he's done on the field, but what he's done off the field for the people of New Zealand as well. – Benji Marshall

I know most kids ran around the backyard and even on the professional footy field imitating and commentating 'SBW' as we offloaded. Any big hit was labelled SBW too. He set the trends on the field with style, flair and success, but the trends he sets now are what makes SBW truly great. Trends like being a great father, great husband, great leader in the community and so much more. What he taught me was that above all, always, Alhamdulillah. – Quade Cooper

If you've got a Williams in your side, you just have to follow him. He will show you the way. It's almost biblical. He may be the best player ever to come out of New Zealand. Everyone wants to watch him play, people idolise him. I love to watch him play. – Ray Warren

Sonny Bill inspired a generation and will continue to inspire.
Grateful for the lessons and our friendship. Proud to have him as
a brother. — Liam Messam

I am grateful that playing sport at the highest level, even with its hardships, has brought such joy to my close ones. And when it comes to compliments, although they are nice to hear, I am always aware of the dangers of taking them to heart. One day's compliments can be the next day's criticisms. But I do care about giving back and doing the right thing. Sport has enabled me to make a difference, and I will keep doing that. The money that came with being an elite sportsperson enabled me to look after my family.

But all that was still in the future . . .

Singapore. London. Biarritz. A long drive to Toulon. A million bucks owed for breach of contract. Playing for Toulon would give me breathing space, and some good people wanted me there and played a big part in my switch to rugby union.

Tana Umaga was one of those good people. Philippe Saint-André, coach of Toulon and future coach of Les Bleus, the French rugby team, and Jonny Wilkinson, England and Lions great and arguably the finest fly half to play the game, were two others.

So, my rugby education started with Tana having the foresight to ring Khoder and say he was serious about offering me a role with Toulon. It had never crossed my mind to play rugby. There had been a little bit of noise in New Zealand about that possibility, but to hear from Tana was mind-blowing. For a man like him to have faith in me really helped settle my nerves and made me seriously consider it.

We spoke on the phone and he said, 'Not only will you make it in rugby, you are going to thrive.' These words gave me such a lift and I could see a way to give myself a break from the dark place I was in. I didn't know who or what I was, only that I was trying to be a better person. Leaving Australia and going to France was the circuit-breaker I needed. In reality, I was running away from myself, but I now know sometimes that is what you need to do to sort out what is important.

Tana offered me a way out of an intolerable situation, and I was so grateful to him for believing in me.

I was a fan of Sonny's from his Bulldog days as a mere eighteen-year-old in that hardest of contact sports playing with and against the hardest of men. I'd heard word of his wanting to leave the Dogs but I wondered if he was serious. I knew of his exceptional talent and could see his work ethic in how he ranged wide and did as much with the little things as he did coming up with big plays, as often as not game-changing.

He didn't just come from nowhere; this Sāmoan boy had everything an athlete could want. Our club owner had never heard of him so I showed him videos and he was immediately interested. But could I get him to switch to rugby union? Seems I did that all right. – Tana Umaga

At a critical time in my life, when I desperately needed someone to look up to and mentor me, Tana Umaga was there. As a man, he is all substance, completely authentic – and of course he has a sporting track record like few others. An Islander, a fellow Sāmoan, an All Blacks captain, he opened the door for me – and I came with massive complications, what with the personal stuff, the code switch, the Bulldogs management after me over my breach of contract. Tana not only believed in me, but he had also told his boss, Mourad Boudjellal, a mega-rich comic-book publisher and the owner of Toulon Rugby Club, that there was this rugby league player who had all the qualities to become a rugby union superstar. (Tana didn't mention this to me at the time; I only found out years later. The eccentric Mourad has since sold Toulon – hailing Tana as his best signing in a side stacked with international stars – and switched from rugby to soccer.) Tana's foresight changed my life. Who knows where I might have ended up if he hadn't called when he did?

Looking back on it, my rugby tutelage in France was second to none. Even though that first year was tough, I flourished, and I played some of the best footy I've ever played, just in a different code. Okay, getting a yellow card in my first game for a shoulder charge was not great. That was just me wanting to impose my physicality. A few games later, though, I got Man of the Match.

The great Jonny Wilkinson was not just my teammate but my tutor, teaching me a new code. A man selfless with his time and, by the way, shy like me – maybe even more so. To me and many others, the best fly half ever to play the game, and he's so shy? Well, what a coincidence. And how lucky was I to fall on my feet like this? My work ethic matched his, and I gladly followed the example he set. With hindsight, I can say quite a few of the international players saw playing in France as the equivalent of a very well-paid holiday, but not me and Jonny. To give you an example, after one of our first training sessions as a team, we had all showered and I had even had some physio. To my amazement, when I was leaving the stadium, Jonny was still out on the field, practising his skills. My admiration for him really started on that day.

Moving from England to play for French team Toulon at the age of thirty was a very big decision for me. I needed a change. I loved how passionate and rugby-loving the club and region were but, above all else, there were a few guys playing there that I couldn't ignore. Sonny Bill Williams was a major one of these. Playing alongside him was a once-in-a-lifetime type of opportunity. So I went and even though we only shared one season, it was well worth it and more.

Our first few pre-season training sessions unfortunately involved me having to row on a machine and sprint up hills next to him. He absolutely destroyed me on both. I remember thinking that this was perhaps the most physically gifted individual I had ever seen. He was built for this sport.

His incredible coordination, power, agility and speed, not to mention his immense level of skill, were obvious to see from the first few games we played together. He just soared above the best the league had to offer in so many ways. He was going to be the future of the game, there was no doubt about it.

What I valued most about our relationship came from getting to know him off the field. I could sense that he was so keen to challenge himself and see what he was capable of. He had an unquenchable thirst for stepping up and giving things a go.

What made it work for me, though, was that he was never afraid to show his vulnerability. By doing so, he expressed total humility and humanity. I knew right then and there that he was going to lead the game into a brilliant new space and that rugby, whatever the code or format, was in very big and exceptionally good hands. – Jonny Wilkinson

I feel like Allah put me in that place to learn from one of the true greats, and he was a great teacher. He was encouraging, and I learned the value of honing my skills and continuously working on them. He's the one who taught me the simple catch and pass that can make the big moments second nature to you. If you put in the training and the preparation, you have the skill set to step up in those big moments in a game. He demonstrated that. Perfect the basics. He practised every kicking skill for hours and hours.

Jonny instilled confidence in me – and remember, at this point I'd still never played a single game of rugby in my life. He used positive language to build me up, and in every game he expressed his faith in me, trying to get the ball into my hands and involving me as much as possible. Then, after a game, he would sit down with me and go through every facet of what had just happened. Our field position meant a different tactic for each situation, rather than my usual 'just play harder' approach. He'd say, 'Sonny, when we get down to their end of the field, we do such-and-such. If we go between our forty and their forty-metre mark and have gone six phases, well, we look for space behind.' I'd go home and write everything down.

The guidelines Jonny gave me stuck throughout my rugby career, that's how good he was, how generous

FINDING A GOOD SPACE

he was – a true great of the game, playing out his last season in Toulon and sharing his knowledge with a rugby novice. He always wanted me with the ball: 'Sonny, go there, it's coming your way.' 'Sonny, step into first-five while I organise out the back.' 'Sonny, head that way!' Next instant, the ball lands in my hands and I have clear space, or just one or two tacklers to beat, with mates running off either shoulder. I couldn't help thinking, *This is unbelievable.* The English and Lions great has so much faith in this shy boy? That's what you call empowerment. And his approach was so simple: trust, have faith, believe in the player outside you.

Philippe was the same. 'Just do your thing, Sonny. One of your biggest attributes is physicality. Use it when and how you like.' That type of buzz. *Okay, how about this?* Shooting out and smashing a guy. Jonny was a mean tackler himself, punched way above his weight – figuratively, I mean, not literally. He was the fairest player; a real English gentleman. But he would try to make even bigger hits than me. He'd do a hit and I'd say, 'That was all right, Jonny.' He would be laughing at me and we would have battles to see who could go hardest. We all know who won that, but it was more a private contest between mates.

As I have said before, when I'm not talking about or playing footy, I'm a man of few words. Footy is business.

Social interaction is a lot harder. Back then, asking someone to go for coffee was just not something I could do.

I'd be thinking, *This is Jonny Wilkinson!* And he was a quiet guy too. Plus, Jonny was always in demand; all his teammates wanted to tap into his knowledge. I would have to wait in line behind five other guys. That is why I say he was such a selfless individual and not for one second up himself. He'd give the rest of us whatever help we asked of him, then go off and hone his own skills. I so appreciated his time and friendship.

One of my fears when I first joined Toulon was that the other players would lack respect for me because I was a rugby union novice, but that proved unfounded. And I mean completely unfounded. They were the opposite; they gave me mad respect. As Tana had predicted, I was thriving in this new game, and the more I played, the better I got. Fast-forward to the last game I played for Toulon – in the losing final against Cardiff – I got Man of the Match.

As soon as Sonny Bill started training with us, I knew my gut feel was right. I saw the traits, how he thinks around issues, his work ethic of not just doing as asked but always doing that bit extra. Not to shine, just for the team. This boy loved being around teammates and was the perfect team man with no big ego, not temperamental.

I remember we had a return-to-play protocol, where you have to observe a set training routine before the season officially starts. His family were visiting and so he missed this routine. What does he do?

There was a median strip near where he lived. It was dark, and he got his father to park his car and turn the headlights on while he ran up and down this median strip. I know now this was a reflection of his dedication to training.

He was well loved and supported by everyone in the Toulon team. And the fans quickly came to love him. They'd not seen a player quite like him. Off the field, he kept pretty much to himself, other than a couple of Muslim mates, one of whom was in our team.

The great Jonny Wilkinson and Sonny Bill were very much alike. Both shy, both extremely hard trainers. They spent hours and hours more than anyone else training, perfecting. JW was a good teacher and his pupil Sonny soaked up everything, both from JW, myself and others he respected. This young man was determined not to just learn a new code but to excel at it. He was always going to be a great. The great players all show the same qualities of determination and being open to learning, not thinking they're better than everyone else. What made him even more special is that he wanted to be a better person. Which is kind of rare in a rugby player of his stature; most feel they don't have to be anything but great on the field.

We had a terrific group of internationals from many countries at Toulon, many of them greats in their own right. But I don't think they'll mind me saying that Sonny Bill stood out as one of a kind. – Tana Umaga

Philippe came and sat beside me on the team bus to ask me to stay on. He promised he would select me to play for France as he would soon be the French coach. Jonny and Tana were also telling me I had what it took to play at international level.

It was such a boost and made me feel it was possible. While in Toulon I had played against international players and certainly felt I got the better of them. But if I was going to play at that level, then I knew I could only ever play for one country: New Zealand.

* * *

There were a lot of good things happening professionally in that year in France, but on a personal level there was more darkness than light. I wanted to succeed so badly. In the early days, the pit of depression was at its worst. I would wake up with migraines and I now know why: everything was about me. I had decided to commit to becoming a Muslim, but that didn't mean I was transformed into a new person overnight. There was still an inner voice saying,

Me, me, me. Everything I was doing was still all about me, not something bigger than myself. I was grateful for what was happening to me with those three legends right behind me. But even a professional player has more private time to themselves to think, often brood on things.

After the first French season ended, I went back to Australia and spent six weeks in boxing camp – not just with Khoder, but with other Muslim brothers. We'd go for walks, do our prayers. I was starting to understand how necessary it is to be in a positive environment. So, when I returned to France in 2009 for my second season, I had a different mindset. I was no longer all about me. While of course I always wanted to succeed and continually improve, I was realising the importance of gratitude, being grateful for everything that comes my way and recognising something bigger than myself.

I loved it over there in Toulon; loved playing with international legends. One of the surprises was how the Toulon fans embraced me. And the more and better I played, the more they loved me. It was humbling and uplifting at the same time. And, of course, the people loved us Top 14 rugby players like we were their own sons. Toulon people love their rugby so much they have a statue of a rugby ball! I'm embarrassed to say this, but in Toulon there is one of those 'Bring Back Buck' things, but with my name. (For those who don't know, it's a New

Zealand thing; when the great All Blacks captain Wayne 'Buck' Shelford was dropped by selectors in 1990, fans started turning up to games with signs reading BRING BACK BUCK.) My first year after playing for the All Blacks, I visited Toulon and went to a match. The club got me to walk the ball out for kick-off and the crowd went crazy. It's a special place, Toulon, especially for the rugby community.

I wasn't just thriving on the field; I was starting to blossom socially, too. I love the French people, but I gravitated to the North Africans and Africans. Toulon is in the south of France, so we were near the tip of North Africa and I met people from Morocco, Algeria, Tunisia. There were people from all over. I'd brought my brother Johnny over, and we became good friends with a Tunisian family.

In that second year, I became even closer to that Tunisian family, who I'm still in contact with today. They helped me to become a better Muslim just through the example of the selfless way they lived and the kindness they shared with so many. I played with a Muslim guy, too: Olivier Missoup. We became really close and roomed together, said our prayers together. He understood my struggles, too. It was really cool to have a kind of soulmate. We went to the mosque together and talked at length. I am also still very close to him today.

Mum, Dad, Johnny and me. Back then, Mum and Dad's mixed relationship would have raised a few eyebrows.

Family and sport were what mattered to me when I was young. Mum kept this clipping of me at age eleven from the local paper. I dreamed of playing professional rugby league and of representing New Zealand in the Olympics.

Mum, Johnny, me, Denise and Niall.

There were five in the bed (the four of us, and our mate Toby) . . . And no wallpaper on the walls.

Nan always had my back. And she paid for my very first sporting trip to Australia.

At fourteen, I was training hard to play in the NRL.

Mum and me at my graduation.

Me and Denise.

My big bro.

Me and my old man, John Senior.

Me and Nan – I miss her.

Johnny, Niall, Denise and me.

Johnny, Mum and me.

Making my debut with the Canterbury
Bulldogs in 2004 was a dream come true,
and winning the premiership that year was
awesome. But, off field, I was about to
head into some dark times.

Reni Maitua, Willie Tonga and me with the 2004 premiership trophy.

Tana Umaga, me and Jonny Wilkinson: I was taught rugby union by the best.

Me and my Toulon teammates.

Moise, Karem and me.

Me and Khoder Nasser.

Training with Tony Mundine.

With my NZPBA Heavyweight
Championship belt.

Fighting Francois Botha.

Anthony Mundine, me and Quade Cooper
and the WBA International belt.

Referee Lance Revill calling an end to my fight against Clarence Tillman for the
NZPBA Heavyweight Championship.

Going back to New Zealand, I had my sights set on one goal: to play rugby with the All Blacks. I played a great season with the Crusaders and then I joined the Chiefs, where I had one of the best experiences of my sporting life. With the mighty Kieran Read (above left), and my mid-field partner at the Crusaders, Robbie Fruean (above right).

The winning Super Rugby Chiefs side.

The support I got from all around the world was awesome. The fans in Cape Town (above) were among the best.

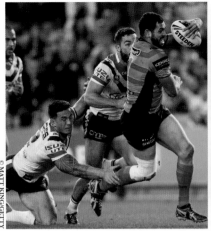

Greg Inglis bumping me off to score
the first try of our big game in 2013.

In 2013, I came back to Australia to play for the
Sydney Roosters. That year would see me play
in another premiership-winning team and Nick
Politis would present me with the Roosters
Players' Player award.

The forming of these relationships really helped in my off-field life.

I don't need to tell you about the quality of this rugby player. He was physically impressive and technically incredible. A player like this you want to share more time with. It is nice to discover you share something in common and, for us, that was a religion about values of respect and sharing.

Sonny came to spend the end-of-year break with me and my family in Paris. This was the first time we were able to be together outside of Toulon.

Sonny met my mother and my family cocoon. I also took pleasure in showing him around my hometown of Paris. We also shared prayers in different mosques in Toulon.

Most of all, I met a friend of rare humility who has great respect for people and who takes time to learn about the history of the people he meets. This is a rare quality these days and not what you would expect of a sports superstar.

Sonny can find himself in a large villa or a small studio. It makes no difference to him. He has the values of sharing and does not give importance to material things. Once I stopped by his hotel where the All Blacks were staying and he gave me some training gear. This is typical Sonny.

In our younger days we were both a bit, shall we say, restless. Today, we're both dads of three and four. Sonny has been important in my personal and spiritual development, and his

I only had two drinking episodes the whole time in France, so it wasn't like I was mixing – as in, wining and dining – with your typical French people. But living there did broaden my horizons. Family visited me, including my dad and his new wife who came to stay with me for a while, which was great.

> I was worried when Sonny left the Bulldogs, and I had talked to him about it. But I knew what was happening, and that he was struggling. I knew from when he was a young age that Sonny had what it took to play in the NRL and I was so proud every time I saw him play because he put everything into the game. He's always been like that. When I was coaching his brother's team, Sonny would turn up to train with the older boys because he wanted to push himself harder. I was confident that one day he'd play rugby league for New Zealand. But when he told me he was leaving league to play rugby union, I was surprised. And then when he made the All Blacks team, I was shocked, but I shouldn't have been. Sonny has big cojones and a big heart, and he backs himself when it matters. All his effort and his strong work ethic paid off. The first game he played with the All Blacks was in England and I watched on the TV back home in Australia with my wife. When he ran out on the field, I cried. I was so proud and happy for him.

influence continues to this day and into the rest of my life. May Allah protect my brother and his family. – Olivier Missoup

I went over to visit Sonny in France and I could see the change since he'd left Australia. He'd got himself into a good space with good friends around him and I knew he was going to be okay. I didn't know at the time that he would become the sporting star he would, and end up representing New Zealand in rugby league, rugby union, rugby sevens and make an Olympic team, but I was proud of him even without those achievements. All I want is for my kids to be happy and thrive. – John Senior

Dad was right, I was happy. Travelling to other cities, I saw how people in different parts of the country lived, how proudly different from each other they were. I loved the restaurants, which were all about friendship and conviviality, community.

I travelled around, too. I went down to Barcelona, flew to Morocco, London. Travel opened up my mind even further. All these new people and new experiences helped to take the focus off myself and I learned there was more to life than just sport – unlike in Australia, where rugby league is all-encompassing. There, I was sucked into the big footy machine, whereas in Europe, rugby is big but not massive. They're just about all mad soccer fans.

I was living a whole new life, and it was changing me.

* * *

One time, I was travelling to Marrakesh with Khoder and the plane hit the worst turbulence I had ever experienced. It was like in the movies when the plane suddenly drops, people get thrown around and hit their heads and people cry out and start praying loudly in desperation. Like my mum, I had a fear of flying but unlike her, I had learned to manage the terror most of the time. That day, the terror was overwhelming. I was sure we were about to die. I looked over at Khoder and he was so composed and calm and when he saw my face he started laughing. I couldn't believe it. I asked him why he wasn't scared and he told me: 'My trust in Allah.' His faith meant he wasn't afraid.

Two months later, Olivier and I were with the team travelling to a game in a private plane and we again hit really bad turbulence. The plane was juddering and falling before climbing back up to a higher altitude and then falling again. People were screaming and the boys were terrified. Something happened in that moment, and I felt this incredible calm settle over me. I wasn't scared and I just thought, *If it is my time, then it is my time*. I started to silently thank Allah and gave thanks for my life, what is called making Dua in the Islamic faith. I looked over at Olivier as our teammates wrestled with their fear and he was like me, calmly accepting whatever happened. We looked at each other and had this mad connection as we realised we both were unafraid. I have never been scared of flying since then. I put my trust in Allah.

Everything had changed for me and I was so grateful to be learning and experiencing things outside what I had known up until then. Everything was new and different, even the old buildings were unlike anything we have in New Zealand and Australia. My favourite place to eat was an Algerian restaurant, run by a Muslim brother, and I could tell he was struggling because all the busy restaurants were on a strip down by the beach. I'd always go there and have my couscous and a bit of lamb, and sometimes it would be just me and the owner. We'd talk, he in his broken English, about his life and his kids and family and I would share with him stories about my life in New Zealand. I just felt this connection, like I did with the Tunisian family I mentioned. I'd often choose to sleep on the floor of their cramped house rather than sleep in my big mansion up in the hills with fantastic views.

One of the sons of the Tunisian couple, Moise, had become a good friend of mine. I had met him at a club during my first year in Toulon: he was working in the cloakroom at the time, taking people's jackets and coats. I wasn't drinking but I still had that attachment to the party life. We were both wanting to be better people and I'd go into the club with the boys, then hang out with Moise in the cloakroom. We'd sit there and have mad yarns and talk about life, our struggles, while my teammates were having a rip-roaring time on the booze next door. We became very close.

Then in my second year, 2009, when my mentality had done a 180-degree turn and my focus was just on playing good footy, I ended up spending a lot of time with Moise's family. His mum would feed me to bursting. Cholesterol levels in that house would have been through the roof! They lived in a one-bedroom place: Mum, Dad and five kids. Materialistically, they didn't have much, yet they were so grateful to Allah for what they had and happily shared food with me, a foreigner. Just their specialness as a family drew me in. And as they became more important to me, I introduced them to my friends. I wanted to share my life and the people who meant a lot to me. It is what we all do. And a beautiful thing happened from that. A close Australian friend's sister ended up marrying Moise's younger brother, Karem. They now have a lovely family of their own and live in Brisbane. We are still very close. I kind of opened the pathway for that brother to have a different life.

I consider Sonny like a brother from another mother, not just a friend. Sonny is a better human than he is an athlete. Simple and humble.

He was looking for balance when he got here to Toulon. He found it in faith and family. Life is made of chance meetings, as happened to us.

Sonny was up for helping all the time. He'd take my mum shopping or just come and visit the kids in the centre I worked for and play basketball and PlayStation with them.

I live in a tough area but that was not important to him. He would come down from his beautiful villa with its magnificent view of the city to join me and my family.

After I started staying with him, when I read articles about him, it was as if the person the articles were talking about did not exist. He has never changed, he has always been the same; he really is that person, true to himself, to his principles, to his faith.

His parents gave him principles and that is what brought us together. His whole family is like that, brother Johnny and his twin sisters. Those of us lucky enough to know him feel privileged. – Moise

Once it got out that I was now Muslim, the word spread like wildfire in the Muslim community. 'Sonny Bill is a Muslim and he's playing for Toulon.' Not that I'd made a statement about it; they'd just noticed me at the mosque every week. I actually wasn't ready to go public at that stage; I was still fighting a few demons. But the seeds were planted in my soul, ready for the most beautiful flowers to grow.

One improvement was that I wasn't drinking in my second year. That didn't affect my relationship with Tana or the boys in any way. I knew my path. I was in a really good space and didn't touch alcohol. I would still go out with the boys. I didn't say to them, 'I'm not drinking because I've become a Muslim.' But it was probably pretty obvious, seeing as I was hanging out a lot with Olivier, the other Muslim guy in our team. Tana never said a word to indicate he was aware of the path I was on. I know he respected my work ethic and my constant drive to be a better player, and that was what mattered.

It was tough telling Philippe at the end of my contract in 2010 that I wouldn't be taking up his offer to play for France, even though I could name my price. I was sorry to say goodbye to Tana, but I know he understood. When I left Toulon to head back home to pursue an All Blacks jersey, he took me aside and said, 'Here is my last Test jersey – now go and get yours.'

The lessons I learned from Tana Umaga in those two years have stayed with me. As a coach, Tana always kept it simple. For instance, with defence, I kept looking for the perfect answer. But I was overthinking it. When looking at the opposition's attacking set-up, Tana explained, just step back and ask the guy who is on the inside of you and the guy on the outside of you who they are going to tackle, and then take the one left. Simple, but very effective. It allowed me to be very physical and to play without hesitation. Throughout the rest of my career, I stuck with that approach, simplifying things. It sometimes seemed to me that the higher I went in rugby, the more overcomplicated the coaches would make it. But I've always felt that keeping it simple works best. It ain't a chess game out there. To this day, when I'm helping out coaching youngsters, I really try to implement that mindset: simplicity, simplicity, simplicity. Times three, just in case you missed it!

The other thing Tana really encouraged was my physicality. That's an Islander thing. Don't suppress your natural instincts. Philippe and Jonny Wilkinson gave me the same message.

Giving me his Test jersey says it all about how Tana regarded me. That gesture is still one of my best memories.

* * *

I mentioned briefly above that I dragged my brother Johnny over to France with me. You'll probably have noticed by now how important Johnny's support has always been to me. When we were working together on this book, Alan Duff talked to him about how he felt about supporting me and about his own footy career potential. Johnny knew he was a good player. But he also knew there were heaps of guys in his team just as good. He lacked the will that I had shown from a young age. That's why I'd play in my age group then go and play another game in his age group – the experience of playing older, bigger, meaner guys really helped prepare me for the big league – whereas he and his mates would play a game and then look ahead to where they'd party. They drank and smoked weed. I wasn't blind to their off-field behaviour, and I am not making moral judgements, but I knew that lifestyle wasn't for me, and it never was until I played NRL and discovered the party life.

I saw a lot of fights growing up, between other kids and between adults, and Johnny was one hell of a scrapper. I was the younger brother and could very well have followed in his footsteps, but I vowed to myself I wouldn't be like that. Even as a teenager, I was determined to stay focused on my rigid training routines and keep that dream alive of one day buying Mum a house. Throughout the age groups, I'd always get the boys on the team to do extra training. That kind of enthusiasm is something you're born with. Keeping it up is the hard part.

I've been lucky that, through all the ups and downs, I've had my brother there to support me. First he joined me in Sydney, then in France. When I left Toulon for New Zealand and moved on to Christchurch to play for Canterbury, he came too. And he's joined me in other ways. He watched my conversion to Islam and one day in France asked to come with me to a mosque. He's converted now, too, so we're still on a shared journey and he has my back always. That was such a special moment when my uso asked to come to masjid with me and made his sha'hada (became a Muslim).

That kind of support is so important – and, equally, a lack of support from those around you can have devastating consequences, as I discovered in my early years in Sydney. I had to make some huge changes to my life to get to the good place I found myself in after a couple of years in Toulon. Back in 2007, I was in the opposite space, in what's called the party life but should be called the toxic life. Cocaine, painkillers, prescriptions, women, alcohol. I was dabbling in it all while learning about the media, how it can both build you up and knock you down, and you have no control over which way it'll go. Though, to be fair, we sportspeople can be silly or unwary enough to feed them fuel to set the fire alight.

The reactions of the clubs often increase the damage done to players rather than supporting them. Often, when their players are caught doing something stupid (I am not talking criminal here), the club apologises and dumps the blame on the player, when in many cases we're talking about an unsupported or misguided youth in a bad culture rather than someone who's inherently bad. There are plenty of examples of players getting drunk and doing things that are stupid, yes, but not violent or abusive or harmful to anyone else – and yet it becomes a black mark against their name. I think of my own DUI charge. That was foolish and dangerous. But a player in a tipsy running race or falling asleep in a club or a cab shouldn't be front-page news and doesn't really warrant an apology, does it?

This is not to say that club administrators are uncaring and self-serving, nor that the media are all wrong and bad. But they are part of the world any young sportsperson has to navigate and you make a misstep at your peril. You have all this fame and money that's supposed to be making you feel so cool and on top of the world. People – especially the media – expect you to be a role model. But how can you be if acclaim comes at the age of eighteen or nineteen? Neuroscientists say the brain isn't even fully developed yet at that age. I am not making excuses for violence or assault; that is different. You know that is wrong early. But behaviour that hurts no-one should not be treated as a major crime.

The bad behaviour that is so often pilloried can be more than just youthful stupidity; it can be a sign of deeper problems. Is a 'role model' allowed to feel depressed? Have mad moments of ecstasy followed by dark despair? This is not how the success script is written. I know

I struggled with the attention. When I was eighteen, I'd be out in public and people would want a photo with me, ask me to sign their footy shirts; they'd say nice things to me, call me to the front of the club and restaurant queues. Suddenly I was a public figure – how is a shy boy supposed to cope with that? That's not in the script either, and I had no-one to guide me. So I found my own ways to deal with it. By having a smoke before I went out or a couple of sleeping tablets to relax me, I was trying to take the fear away. I didn't think about the consequences – that it can make you drowsy and lead to you doing stupid stuff, like finding yourself asleep on the floor at some stranger's pad. And that's just small stuff; the consequences can be a whole lot worse. One time, I went on a bender that lasted from Friday night to Monday morning. The only reason I came home is I knew I had a surgery appointment at 11 am. I don't remember anything about the operation except waking up and finding my girlfriend crying next to the bed as the doc really gave it to me, telling me I had so many drugs in my system I could have died.

It is not easy for me to open up like this. But I feel it is important to be honest, and I hope younger people take notice of my mistakes and avoid making the same ones themselves.

At the end of 2007, playing with the Dogs, I had a moment of clarity; I knew I could not continue down this road. I decided I couldn't go on living like this, feeling like I couldn't control my desires or break out of the vicious circle I was stuck in. Depression was just one of the feelings I would carry every morning-after. Yet even as I was deteriorating mentally, my footy form had got better; it had not suffered in any way. We were going into the semi-final against the Eels and I felt full of confidence, determined to make this a good game for me.

In the first five minutes I get involved, make a couple of statement tackles, go looking for the ball, make a break, do a mad offload to our fullback, who sets up Willie Tonga, who runs, trips, pops up a beautiful ball to Matt Utai, who scores in the corner. You see how I'm not the troubled, lost guy on the field?

Two minutes later, the Eels' Nathan Hindmarsh, who everyone had been talking up before the match, decides to run the ball up. Okay, I'm gonna smash him, but he's a smart old hand, and as I swing my arm at him, he ducks his head, right on my forearm. My arm goes dead.

I get up, thinking, *Something is wrong here*, but I keep trying to play . . . No, I can't. I've broken my arm. I tried to come back in the second half, said to the team helpers, 'Just bandage me up, I'm going back out.' My first run with the ball, I couldn't even move my arm. I get tackled, feel something else click, or snap, in my wrist. I get up, walk across the field and know it's bad. The depression hits before I even leave the ground. I'm a man who is defined by his game and it has been taken away from me. I am worthless. I feel empty. There's one way I know of to banish that feeling: I start drinking, kidding myself I am still The Man, even though inside, deep down, I'm feeling a huge sense of loss. I know the serious injury means I'm out – again.

In those days, taking alcohol and drugs was how I dealt with the dark times; it was the only way I knew. I go back to my first major injury in 2005, only my second year in NRL, when I did my knee and was out for the rest of the year. I was living with another injured player, Willie Tonga, and we just partied. Every day of the week except Mondays. Willie never touched drugs, but I did. I touched everything going that was supposed to give bodily pleasure.

Come Monday, it's 6 am and Willie and I were sitting in the car with training due to start in a few hours, asking ourselves what had we done, where had we been? Who were these women in the car with us? At least Willie had his Christian faith, so he'd say a little prayer then off we'd go to training. But because of that psychology of mine, I never felt like I belonged to the team if I was out injured. I have to believe I am contributing in order to feel like I belong. I didn't think about being on full pay during that time. I can't remember feeling guilty about that. I guess it was just my contract. I am sure the club knew I was partying all the time; they just didn't say anything. It seems the clubs only get worried when something goes public and the media get a hold of it.

When Willie and I flatted together, we'd go partying, and yet I remember going past his room and he'd be sitting there reading the Bible. I don't know what it was, but I felt this connection to God when I saw the calming effect his Christianity had on him. That was probably a faint signal trying to awaken my own spirituality. I never once made fun of his religious belief, not even as a joke between mates. It felt too big and important to make light of it.

By the time I headed home from France, though, I had come a long way, in my footy and in my life. Khoder Nasser was a major influence; he really helped me to get my head right. He talked straight to me, did not hold back on criticising my off-field behaviour or pointing out the odd mistake on the field. If I messed up off-field, he'd ask, 'What are you doing, mate? Seriously, Sonny, pull your head in.'

No-one else had ever pulled me up like that. When I was in the company of Khoder and the people he surrounded himself with, I saw it was a healthy way to live: no drugs, no alcohol, no women, yet lots of laughs. He was someone I could bounce ideas off, someone I could talk to about things I didn't share with anyone else. He became a close confidant, with his blunt honesty, sincerity, loyalty and integrity. I feel lucky that when I needed it, he helped to show me a better path. I am grateful I had the courage and the strength in myself to listen to the message from the One God when I most needed it. I realised I needed boundaries and discipline to be a better man and I found that in my faith. Sometimes I wonder where I'd be if I hadn't been supported by the strength of Islam and turned my life around.

CHAPTER 6

You are just a caretaker

I have been talking about myself for too long now, so I'm going to take a break and let my big bro, Johnny, share his thoughts about his little brother – though I reserve the right to dispute any of it!

* * *

Sonny and I competed with each other back in the day. I'd ask: 'How many tries did you score, Sonny?' 'Two.' 'Well, I scored three.' Or it would be vice-versa. We were a real competitive family, Dad and us four kids.

Sonny was pretty driven from day dot; he had the speed and that little sidestep. Bit of a cheeky little fella, and we could never catch him because he just sidestepped away, kind of like this taunting way of staying just out of your reach. He had style even at a young age.

Knowing him like I do, and seeing him play at the top for nearly twenty years, he never got scared of it that I could see. He loves the big occasions, and the bigger it is, the more he rises to it. I remember him as a kid playing and, honestly, it was like a man against boys. He just stood out as he went through the grades. He even stood out when cadging a game with us older kids, which we didn't mind because he was a hell of a player.

Then he went to first grade and I thought, *Here we go, this is the real big league, his Bulldogs debut.* His first or second touch he makes a big break, sets up a try, scores one himself. His name was all over the papers and on television the next day. A 'new star is born' kind of thing. Yet despite his amazing fame, the rest of the family and I still see the same old Sonny we've always known. Humble, loving, down to earth, great sense of humour and loves to tease or be teased.

He's my little brother, and I had our mother's protective streak as far as he was concerned. At our primary school once, someone came running up to tell me one of the tough boys at the school had given Sonny a hiding. At lunchtime I gave that boy a hiding in return. I still have that protective instinct today. When I've watched or read what some of the media have had to say about him over the years, naturally I'd get mad. Because their comments do *not* match the countless videos I've watched of him over and over. My bro was never a player 'past his best', 'over the hill' or 'chalky'; he was never 'Money Bill'. My brother is a freak of nature like none ever seen before.

Only a handful had it in for him, but that doesn't make it any less hurtful and infuriating. I think they're resentful because he's always done things his way, like the back-and-forth code switches, and has triumphed each time. They don't like his total independence. Some may even hate that with every code switch, he hits the top. Not the middle and never the bottom. The *top*.

One journo said he shouldn't be picked for the Rugby World Cup because in his last Test his form was poor. How could he say that when it just wasn't true? I sometimes wonder if him being a Muslim might be a problem for his Caucasian Kiwi critics. I've watched footy all my life and, listening to the commentators, you'd think you were watching two different games when you hear what they say about him. I'd heard of how 'Super' Sid Going, playing back in the 1960s and 70s, used to say that as a Māori he had to play twice as good to get selected in the All Blacks. Maybe it's the same mindset with Sonny being Muslim: *You better prove yourself to us, boy.*

I know Sonny changing from league to union upset more than a few people, especially when he proved a big star at the new code. Sonny changed both codes forever, with his offloads adopted all over the world.

We're a pretty private family and that includes Sonny. He loves our family environment and never, I mean *never*, boasts about his on-field exploits; doesn't say a word about it unless to laugh at something he did. I've heard people talk about him and I never said I was his brother. Just had a laugh even when they

141

criticised him. I don't want people talking to me just because I'm Sonny Bill's brother. I want them to talk to me for who I am, not someone with a famous brother.

Do I have any regrets not making more of my league career? Not really. In our team of seventeen-year-olds, there were eleven guys just as good as each other. Sonny was way better, and he was two years younger than us. We all had talent, but who of us had Sonny's drive?

I got into trouble as a teenager. Sonny never did. I got a six-month suspension for whacking someone in a game when I was sixteen. I broke the jaw of this big Island boy who wanted a fight with me. I was banned from all contact sports, and once that happened it was the end of league for me and I went down the wrong track. But at least I knew enough to warn Sonny off following my path.

I was in New York playing rugby for about eighteen months, then came home and hurt my neck in a car crash. So, I was a bit down over that when Sonny called to see if I wanted to join him in Toulon. I loved it over there. My older daughter speaks fluent French now.

On my dad, I'll only say he had a tough life that hardened him. To see him now, the alcohol is gone and he's a cool grandad; my kids, Sonny's and our sisters' kids all love him to bits. I'm a bit soft with my kids, more of a friend than a father, and I let them get away with too much. I don't need to hit them; I just raise my voice and that's enough. Like with my teenage daughter, she's at that point where she wants to try things out. I'd rather she felt free to come and say, 'Dad, I've done something wrong' than be too scared to approach me. I want my kids in that frame of mind where they think they can tell their dad anything and it'll be okay. She might get a telling-off, but she'll have a loving, understanding ear.

I remember Sonny from a young age would train with his team then run to catch the end of our training. It could be hosing down, he didn't care, he just wanted to get stuck into more training. Same on Saturday game days: my little bro was so greedy for game time he was prepared to play boys two years older, and at that age there is a difference in strength and maturity. No problem to him; he could hold his own. I think us being half-caste, we weren't fully accepted either by the full Sāmoans or by the whites. So we had to go twice as hard to prove ourselves. That's how I learned to fight. I was the whitest Sāmoan among all my cousins, and they used to tease us. I just went up the road and learned from a boxing trainer how to throw a punch and started whacking them. The teasing stopped.

Sonny had the same attitude, except he did it with hard tackles, shoulder charges. Always the next level up, always dominated. He can play like a Mack Truck or like a Ferrari. Even though he's my brother, I know my sport well enough to recognise greatness, the player who can do it all: sidestep, a weaving run, draw them in, a big arm reaches out and – boom. There's the offload he made uniquely his own, the

143

tackling, turnovers, so many moves seen and unseen that change a game.

He goes from top of the rugby league tree to rugby union in Toulon, back to New Zealand to play for Canterbury and, without playing a single Super Rugby game, goes straight into the All Blacks. Wins a Rugby World Cup in 2011, the following year joins the Chiefs and they win the title. Who's their stand-out player? Him, of course. Shall I go on?

Okay, 2013, back to league for the Sydney Roosters and they win the grand final, and again he was the stand-out player. You need any more convincing? Okay, same year, 2013, he plays rugby league for the Kiwis against England. Man of the Match. Back to rugby 2014, back in the All Blacks, in 2015 he's in the World Cup squad, wins a gold medal with a series of offloads and match-winning moves. Gives his medal to a kid. One commentator said he did it to bring all the attention on himself. This is my shy brother, the bro with so much empathy, and that's what is said about him?

I think everyone knows that sports commentators have got their favourites. Meaning, they can't see anyone else, even if someone is doing amazing things in the same game or off the field. One of the many things I learned is to be fair with people. If you're fair with them, then you can stand your ground knowing you've done the right thing.

* * *

Thanks, bro. I'll take it from here and pick up in France.

In my second year at Toulon, everything had changed. The self-indulgent stuff was all behind me. Clean. Free. Unburdened. That desire to be in the All Blacks was even stronger, and not from the traditional base of dreaming of it since I was a little kid. (You already know what my dream was: to buy Mum a house with fancy wallpaper, which I did, and it is the home she still lives in today.) Until I moved to Toulon, I had never given rugby union a thought. League was my one and only game. To tell the truth, I'd had the attitude that union was a softer game, while league was for real hard men. But I discovered otherwise. Like with every sport I've been involved in, I see it as a challenge first and foremost.

I ended my time with Toulon on a high. We were in the European Cup grand final and I scored and the crowd went crazy. It was such a buzz, and being in a much better state of mind in life generally made it all the more enjoyable. I remember getting the ball about thirty metres out, banging off my left foot, right foot, going straight through and scoring the try. I threw the ball into the crowd for joy. Tana was on the bench, and he was jumping up and down. I ran over and gave him a hug and all the bench boys came and hugged me. Even though we lost that last match against Cardiff, it was the same feeling that I would have for the Chiefs in the 2012 Super

Rugby final. In that game, I'd score the try that would seal the win, and then jump up into the stand with the fans as my way of saying thanks for your loyal support, my way of conveying, *We won this for you.*

That was my last game for Toulon. After that, I headed home to see if I could make the All Blacks. Back in New Zealand, Johnny and I visited Mum and our sisters and spent some time with them, then it was off to Christchurch. My first match there was for a local club, Belfast, where I met Bill Bush, the legendary Māori prop and All Blacks enforcer. He was so welcoming to me. My presence drew a massive crowd for a club match; I think around 4000 people. Stats show I made thirteen offloads, twenty-one carries and scored a try in my fifty-minute appearance. It was nice to be back among ordinary folk, where I feel most comfortable.

I played five National Provincial Championship (NPC) games for Canterbury, then was selected for the All Blacks. That was huge. I might not have been a loudly nationalistic type of guy, but that did not mean I valued the jersey any less. I saw it as a question of playing with the best. The All Blacks are the best sporting team in the history of all team sports. So, you have to represent with mana, play at your highest level, because of the All Blacks' history. If you're playing with the All Blacks, you can say you're among the best in your position in the world.

I knew All Blacks status meant a lot for my family, but for me, it meant I was one of the best. So there was big pressure in that sense, but I took great pride in stepping up to that.

They have this saying in the All Blacks: 'You are just a caretaker. Leave the jersey better than you found it.' That is a really humbling way to play. You are forging a path for those to come and honouring all those in whose footsteps you are following. As I played with no sense of self-preservation, I knew it wasn't hard for me to leave everything out on the field. Even if I started on the bench, when I came on, I gave it my all.

I realise that seeing me go from the NPC to the All Blacks must have been a bit strange for my All Blacks teammates. I came with a massive reputation as the party boy who was all about money, someone who did not honour his contracts, was a code- and club-hopper, that sort of thing. I felt I had to remove that stigma, and the best way to do that was play well.

But I also could have an attitude of, *If I've shown you that I can play rugby at a high level and been vulnerable enough to reach out to you, yet you still put that stigma on me, then my levels of respect for you would evaporate.* I've had that mentality since I was a youngster. Maybe it's just self-protection. What I did know was I had come prepared through rigorous training, and from not touching alcohol or putting any other toxic substance in my body.

I've still got that training mindset. Just this year, I wasn't satisfied with my boxing sparring. I didn't get dusted up, yet that's what my mind told me. Three o'clock the next morning, I'm wide awake thinking about that 'failure'. By four, I was back in the gym training. That day I did three sessions.

I had that mindset going into the All Blacks. I remember that first game, at Twickenham against England, running out there and standing in a huddle and looking up to see Jerome Kaino watching me, smiling and nodding. He's smiling at me, like saying, *You're here, bro. I'm right here with you.* I was getting mad energy from him seeming pleased that I was there, and it was just as mad a vibe for me being there with him.

Sonny was the ultimate professional, from how hard he trained to what he ate. It was a huge privilege to see him operate in that space. For me and the other players, watching him was inspiring.

For me, Sonny single-handedly changed the game from how teams defended against the offload. But also in how players wanted to play the game. It all came from him setting the example, with totally original thinking and execution.

But my fondest memories of Sonny aren't on the pitch, it's how giving he was with his time to anything: family, community and those in need. Being a superstar in demand, he would always be willing to give his time to my kids.

As a brother, I not only admire him for what he's done for sport, but for how inspiring he has been through his Muslim faith and being a genuinely great person/leader/father/husband/ brother. The man is a true legend. – Jerome Kaino

Thank you, uso! But it was me who was inspired by my teammates. Look to one side and there's Ma'a Nonu. Over there, Joe Rokocoko, the flying Fijian-born winger. The steady hand of Keven Mealamu. It was such a proud moment because I was remembering how determined I'd been to take up the challenge to make the All Blacks. And suddenly there I was; it was happening for real. On the way to Britain, I'd watched the All Blacks game against the Wallabies in Hong Kong. It was the first time I'd ever seen them play live. The year before, when I was in Toulon, a bunch of us players went to watch them play France in Marseilles. But when we got there, one of the guys had forgotten the tickets! He'd brought a power bill instead of the tickets Tana had got for us. So we stood outside the stadium and listened to the haka, then drove home.

Now, here I was, with not even one Super game behind me, and I was one of them: an All Black. It was a great achievement.

The game went well. I did a few offloads, did my defensive job. Then I hit half a hole and go down real late, look up and there's big Jerome right there to give a mad offload to and he draws an England defender and then passes to Hosea Gear, who scores in the corner. JK runs up and gives me a big hug and I'm so pumped because I belong.

After the game, Ma'a Nonu gave me a tie as a debut player. To think, only two years before I had walked away from rugby league and made the switch to union. Now I was back in Europe, and I'd just had my debut for the All Blacks. It was a special time because I had achieved a goal I had set myself.

I loved the All Blacks' environment, playing with the very best, hearing their thoughts on the game, each of us free to let our voice be heard. Because of my Islamic faith, I am not comfortable supporting alcohol, gambling or bank-based businesses. They are part of my no-go zone when it comes to wearing a sponsor's logo, and the All Blacks totally respected my position.

In the team structure, there are always individuals who stand out for different reasons. Extroverts, funny guys, musical talents, serious dudes, quiet men, loud fellas. I used to love being alone sometimes, just by myself, happy in my own company. But I also enjoyed chilling with the boys and, I have to say, us brown boys naturally gravitate towards each other. It's just how it is with us Islanders and Māori.

* * *

Making the All Blacks' 2011 Rugby World Cup team was another goal achieved and I am really proud of the way I played throughout that whole tournament. I was so happy for my country and my teammates as we achieved something special, beating France 8–7 in the final. I would like to give a special mention to France's captain, Thierry Dusautoir – what a player he was. He almost got them home single-handed. Being awarded the Man of the Match award in a beaten side in a World Cup final was a special feat in itself.

2011 Rugby World Cup Squad

Forwards: Kieran Read, Adam Thomson, Jerome Kaino, Victor Vito, John Afoa, Brad Thorn, Sam Whitelock, Ali Williams, Anthony Boric, Keven Mealamu, Andrew Hore, Corey Flynn, Tony Woodcock, Owen Franks, Ben Franks, Richie McCaw (c.)

Backs: Mils Muliaina, Israel Dagg, Isaia Toeava, Cory Jane, Zac Guildford, Conrad Smith, Ma'a Nonu, Sonny Bill Williams, Richard Kahui, Daniel Carter, Colin Slade, Jimmy Cowan, Piri Weepu, Andy Ellis

Fast-forward four years and I was to achieve another goal, making the All Blacks 2015 Rugby World Cup team. Every time I was given an opportunity, I played exceptionally well. Among my All Blacks teammates, I was thriving on the biggest stage.

2015 Rugby World Cup Squad

Forwards: Kieran Read, Sam Cane, Victor Vito, Jerome Kaino, Liam Messam, Brodie Retallick, Sam Whitelock, Luke Romano, Ben Franks, Owen Franks, Charlie Faumuina, Wyatt Crockett, Joe Moody, Dane Coles, Keven Mealamu, Codie Taylor, Tony Woodcock, Richie McCaw (c.)

Backs: Ben Smith, Julian Savea, Nehe Milner-Skudder, Waisake Naholo, Ma'a Nonu, Conrad Smith, Malakai Fekitoa, Sonny Bill Williams, Daniel Carter, Beauden Barrett, Colin Slade, Aaron Smith, TJ Perenara, Tawera Kerr-Barlow

To beat the Wallabies 34–17 in the final was the first time in World Cup history a team had won back-to-back and retained the Webb Ellis Cup. I'll never forget that game.

Half-time comes and Steve says, 'You ready?'

'Yeah, sure I'm ready.'

I was more than ready – I was pumped! I'm supposed to run out with the team, but I go out early and then the boys come out. 'Bro, you pretty much missed the team talk!' To me, the time for talking was long over. It was time for action.

My second touch was an inside offload to Ma'a for a try. It put us in a commanding lead and, to be honest,

I just wanted to contribute. *Give me the ball, give me the ball*, I remember thinking. Nugget (Aaron Smith) must have been sick of hearing my voice. Allah blessed me to be involved in such a special team. In my opinion, that side will go down as one of the greatest rugby teams in history.

I was rooming with Ma'a for the final week on that tour and we got hold of the trophy and slept with it in our room. We changed into our lavalavas and just floated on a cloud. Ma'a was one of the cleanest guys you could ever meet; he would have everything spick-and-span, and nice scents everywhere. So there's us two Sāmoans in traditional lavalavas, sitting in a room that smelt like a flower garden. And there's the Webb Ellis Cup sitting there gleaming – beaming, it felt like – at us! *We've done it again, bro!* Although there was always a competitiveness between us, I never felt it got in the way of our friendship. I consider Ma'a a close friend for life and I wish we could have partnered up more. I feel like we would have been an unstoppable combination.

* * *

Growing up in a household with little money gave Sonny a special affinity with those less fortunate. That's why he advocates for refugees; he really connects with people whom life has not treated kindly. Part of this concern for others can be seen in the respect he shows his opponents. After the All Blacks beat the Springboks in the 2015 semi-final, Sonny's opposite, Jesse Kriel, was sitting under the goalposts completely dejected. They'd come to that game convinced they'd beat the All Blacks and it had all come crashing down. At that low point, he felt a hand on his shoulder and then Sonny was crouching down beside him, telling him he'd get over this. Sonny embraced his enemy of only minutes before, helped him up. Kriel later said Sonny had every right to be over with his teammates celebrating their victory, yet instead he had stopped to console him, embracing him. That just shows the type of player Sonny is, the calibre of the man. – Khoder Nasser

Sport can bring out the best in people. It can forge bonds and create an understanding, and I have learned a lot from my teammates and from my opponents. I do respect my opponents, and the better they are, the more I respect them. I don't think openly showing that respect is anything to be ashamed of. If anything, it's the opposite. It's part of our Polynesian/Māori culture. Show respect. Though maybe not on the field! My brother Israel Dagg has something to say about that.

Sonny and I were similar in being family oriented. Growing up in big households with all our brothers and sisters meant we loved to have company around us. Me being Māori and him Sāmoan in a predominantly white Canterbury environment definitely drew us closer.

In Cape Town in 2011, playing for the Crusaders against the Stormers, we had a hell of a win. But it came at a cost: I tore the quad of my hip that turned into five months out of action. But typical Daggy, I thought I might as well hit the town and drink myself stupid all night.

A team meeting was called. It turns out I'd been spotted in the lobby, kicking up chaos, and had given us all away. We go into the meeting room and the coaches reveal what they know. I was under the pump, everyone coming at me, left, right and centre. The only thing is, I hadn't been the only one out that night. But I took it on the chin and didn't say a word.

I've got quite emotional by this time. Next minute, Sonny comes and stands alongside me. 'I was out, too,' he told the coach. He stood up and had my back. He didn't have to. I made the dumb decision to be an idiot in the lobby and ruin it for everyone. But Sonny stood up for a brother. No-one else did.

I realised then this guy is a genuine brother, to take some of my heat. Like when I missed selection for the 2015 Rugby World Cup, he came around and sat with me for ages, telling me stuff like, 'This game does not define you.'

What rugby player says that kind of thing? He was right there as a brother, and you never forget times like that. People only get the media version of Sonny. Not the caring and genuine man I know. In fact, the most caring man I've ever met.

Back home in Christchurch, I'm on crutches and Sonny turns up. 'Come on, let's go for a ride.' He'll never forget his friends and family. Always asks after someone's family. A lot of media people portray him as something he is so far from being, you'd think they invented a story and just run with it. They have no idea who the real Sonny is.

The Sonny I know treats everybody the same. Big rugby stars. The cleaner. Ordinary people. He doesn't care. You – all of us – are the same in his eyes.

Playing with him, every time he got the ball, I knew to hang off his shoulder, knowing I'd get the offload. Against Tonga in the Rugby World Cup, I scored from one of his offloads. So many games he set me up for tries.

Playing *against* him when he moved to the Chiefs was another story. Daunting to see the big fella ready to put a monster hit on you.

Wherever he goes he takes people with him; he doesn't say much but we players see his micro-skills, how he is 100 per cent a team man. No secret to his success. He trains like no-one else I've ever seen. Take a look at his 900 abs.

Sonny is a big part of my life. I want people to know the real Sonny. Love you, my brother. – Israel Dagg

Love you too, my uso. Words like this and those connections with my teammates mean a lot, but just like with the 2012 Super Rugby semi-final against Izzy's

156

Crusaders . . . respect? That can wait until after the game! I tried to smash Israel every chance I got. He is one of the finest players New Zealand has produced, and we're mates from Canterbury and Crusaders and All Blacks days. Izzy can pull a laugh out of anything. But on the field? In the heat of battle, there was no time for laughs – that was always my mindset when I played.

That reminds me of something that happened in my first rugby league season in Australia in 2003. I was actually quite shocked when I got there to find there was such a thing as Aussie Islanders (how naive I was). And I was even more shocked to find they didn't seem like us Kiwi Islanders. We showed respect by running hard or smashing each other, but it only went so far, and afterwards, at least in my experience, it was all about love between us Islander players. But on this occasion in 2003, this brother wanted to fight and bring the niggle.

It was different to my norm, but I thought, *Okay, if they're the rules over here, I will have to adapt.* I get tackled by him and I guess he wants to show who is boss, he keeps pushing my head down. I got up and pushed him. So then he tested me with fists up. I have a mad thing about wanting to take down bullies. He was psycho; his eyes were bulging and he'd clearly lost it, but I wasn't going to back down. I had a fleeting thought that maybe I'd bitten off more than I could chew, but that thought never lasts long, not out there in the arena. *Get in first*, I told myself. Which I did, with some good accurate shots. His face was bleeding and his rage had got worse. He wanted to keep fighting. But the ref sent us both off.

I was walking off, thinking it was over now. I didn't want to fight anymore; I was leaving it on the field. Then I heard voices screaming, 'Sonny! Turn around, he's coming!'

I turned and saw this enraged monster coming at me as he stripped off his jersey to reveal a body packed with muscle. Man.

He runs up and I catch him with a perfectly timed left hook – this is before I ever thought of being a boxer. Down he goes and everyone's going mad. The guy's bench jumps up and joins in. One king-hits me, I chase him and reply with a left hook. Johnny was in the melee somewhere, our bench has joined in, spectator fans from both sides are in. Unbelievable.

There was an aftermath long after that and Johnny was not so lucky. He was in this bar one time and these guys were giving him lip because they knew he's my brother. He followed one to the toilet and dropped him. But then my crazy bro comes back to the bar and carries on drinking for an hour or so. When he walked outside there were five guys waiting for him. But at least it was fists, not guns and knives like nowadays.

But that's not how we do it where I come from. For us, Islanders and Māoris playing against each other, especially at the highest levels, is a special buzz. Many of us come from the exact same background. Playing against each other is special because we know it's going to be hard, but it's only our way of showing respect to one another. If we play Sāmoa or Tonga, our reputation doesn't mean a thing. I've played some of my toughest games against those teams.

And my teammates and their respect mean the world to me. Over the years, I have forged friendships that will last for life. I won't attempt to name them all, out of fear of missing someone out, but Sammy Whitelock was one. Although I struggled socially down south, he had a way of making me feel at home. A family man who will definitely go down as one of the great, if not the greatest, locks to have played the game (even if I will always be stronger than him in the gym).

2010 was my first year with the Canterbury squad. I knew who Sonny Bill was and had heard of his Bulldogs and Kiwis credentials and his switch to rugby in France. He came up and introduced himself and we hit it off from there. I have a memory of a Ranfurly Shield match and us up 20–10 but we could not get out of our own half. Sonny did that, single-handedly.

I soon learned he was something special – we all did. He had
the ability to change a game. In any team sport there are just a
handful of people with that ability, with that X-factor. He had the
skill to break a game open.

Both of us were keen to achieve our long-term goals. We
started our first Test match together. We played for Canterbury,
the Crusaders and the All Blacks together and became close.
In our sport, we're competitive. Yet Sonny's training still stood out
and a lot of players followed his example.

He understood what he had to do off the field; he was
approachable and loved to discuss everything about the game.
Yet he was so modest and humble. Just not in the gym! Where he
compared himself to everyone in weights and aerobics, whatever.
And when he got the better of someone he joked and teased and
took the mickey. Sonny Bill Williams is a very special man, both
as a player and a person. – Sam Whitelock

Another close brother, Liam Messam, I'm sure won't
mind me saying that one of the reasons we connected
was I could see through his front, see the frailties behind
the tough facade. He was our leader in the 2012 Chiefs,
the man we all looked up to, who led by example. And
he put aside his personal issues for his team brothers.
We went from being a bunch of misfits to competition
champions in one season. Recently, Hunga spoke publicly
about the mental struggles he faced, how he was trying

to be that quintessential Māori warrior while inside he was in great pain. If someone like Hunga can be honest about his struggles, then I am not ashamed of admitting my own.

***

I would go on to play with the All Blacks until 2019. That last tour was a whirlwind and I am so grateful for it all.

When I look back at who has influenced me and who helped me become who I am, I always think of Johnny. If I didn't have my brother's support, I definitely would not be where I am today.

He was no angel, but he is a good man, especially with his kids. Okay, if they make him mad he'll call me, and though we don't talk about the actual situation, we're on the phone kind of exchanging feelings by mental telepathy. He asks for advice without asking for advice, if you get my drift.

I've heard him say to his son, 'Don't worry about that missed tackle. You did ten massive hits today. Son, as long as you're happy, as long as you understand who gave you your skills – it wasn't me. It was Allah. Be happy when you play no matter what.'

You might be thinking, what has this got to do with rugby? Well, I think it's who a person is behind the player image that is most important. If I wrote this book and did not acknowledge those who helped lift me up, then forget my reputation as a player. That would make me a selfish, egotistical man all about me, myself and I, and not worthy of anyone's respect.

CHAPTER 7

A memory buried in a shallow grave

When I was in France, I'd had the feeling that I could compete against the very best and that's when I started to believe in myself as a rugby player and yearn for more competition. Which led me to New Zealand, of course. Then to make the All Blacks and play well obviously felt good. But inside I was still carrying that same old desire to keep improving.

In those years, I was living a really clean life, studying the game, learning, but still retaining my Islander physicality and flair, and it was all starting to come together. We had a weighted ball at home in Christchurch. Johnny was living with me and every night we would do fifty catch and passes each side just to give me confidence throwing a long ball. But I got an injury called osteitis pubis, which caused pain low in the stomach and groin, from over-training.

So what do I do? Train, and then go home and train some more. My dedication levels were extremely high; I'd do extra video sessions, soaking up everything. And my faithful bro, Johnny, he was there with me all the way.

* * *

On 4 September 2010, Johnny and I were at home in our unit in Christchurch – it was the day after I'd played my first game for Canterbury. At about 4.30 am, I was woken by this terrible roar. I hit the light and saw the whole room was rocking from side to side.

My door swung open and there's my brother standing there in his undies; I remember watching his stomach going from side to side with the room. We were both in shock. Being woken abruptly in the middle of the night to find the world shaking and shuddering is a pretty full-on experience. We were upstairs and my brain, realising an earthquake had struck, was assessing if it was safer up here or out on the street – if we could even walk downstairs.

When it kept going, we decided the street was a safer place to be and made our way outside (once Johnny found some pants!). It was scary and there was a lot of damage to the building. We learned later it was a 7.1 magnitude earthquake and that two people were injured and one person died from a heart attack. Later, there were aftershocks, but things got back to normal pretty fast for me. And then, five months later, it happened again – but worse.

On 22 February 2011, at 12.51 pm, I was doing recovery in the pool with teammate Tu Umaga-Marshall in central Christchurch, just down from the apartment hotel I was staying in because my unit had been rendered uninhabitable by the September 2010 earthquake. Suddenly, the whole place started going off. I mean, *off*!

Our hot pool was going from side to side, and someone shouted at us to stay in the pool. Don't ask me why. The shaking was so violent I swear our brains were sloshing madly in our skulls. Who can think in a situation like that? One guy jumped out of the pool and tried to run, but he was staggering like he was on drugs or something.

The big pool was full of aqua-joggers and the water had turned to waves. It was overlooked by big glass windows, and I was waiting for them to shatter and come down onto the heads of the aqua-joggers. Man, it was more than surreal. You couldn't make a movie of it. As soon as it stopped, I knew I was in a state of shock, as was everyone else. To this day I can still feel how it affected me. It's something you can't explain unless you've been in a major earthquake. It's like a memory buried in a shallow grave.

Tu jumped out and ran to his phone because his kids were at the movies at the other end of town. He was trying to call his wife, but he couldn't get through. We didn't know then that the phone towers were either down or so badly damaged they weren't working.

We got changed and ran outside to witness destruction everywhere. Tu was already worried sick for his kids' safety and in an even worse state when we saw the devastation. We were just walking around in a state of total shock. On the street, a whole row of verandahs had come crashing down and we could see a leg sticking out of a pile of rubble, a hand. It was just awful. And my mate was just beside himself with worry for his family. Eventually, we got the good news that they were unharmed.

It was as if the whole world had been turned upside down then thrown from a great height. It was pure mayhem. We saw what looked like a tablecloth laid over someone who was obviously dead. I heard crying, screaming, groaning; it was like a scene out of some horrific nightmare.

About twenty people were gathered around a truck, trying to listen to the radio. The ground had turned to liquid in some places. Homes, schools, shops and office buildings were destroyed and roads, bridges, power and phone lines badly damaged. I could go on a lot more about what I saw, but the event has been covered enough in the media, by writers and historians, and I find the horror hard to describe.

At first, I was really worried because my sister Niall was in town. But because all the phones were down, I couldn't reach her. That kind of sick anxiety is something you don't ever want to feel. Some people had that same feeling, but it didn't come right for them. They never got to see their friends and family again. It turned out Niall and Johnny and everyone I knew was okay, but we would soon learn that 185 people had died and nearly 200 were seriously injured. So many people were left homeless, businesses had been destroyed. I know we all felt so helpless and the fear of another quake was very real.

I wanted to help in some way, and not long after an idea occurred to me: I could hold a boxing match to raise money to help with the recovery. Though it took a while to organise, eventually we made it happen. It was held in West Auckland on 5 June 2011, on a weekend when Canterbury had a bye. I fought Tongan heavyweight Alipate Liava'a. I won that fight after six rounds, but more importantly I was able to personally donate $100,000 to the Christchurch Earthquake Appeal.

Looking back on it, I feel proud to have contributed. It's a way of sharing pain others have gone through and for us lucky, unscathed people to be grateful. After the earthquake, our rugby ground – the famous Lancaster Park – was no longer usable, and having to play games away from home meant seeing less of my mum. She was terrified to fly but now she had something else to fear. Many people, including Mum, were scared of another earthquake. And with our schedule completely changed, there just wasn't the time between games and training to get to her place. I did manage to see her briefly, though, which I think Mum appreciated!

Funny, when John Arthur and Sonny Bill got back from France, I thought at least my children were closer and safe. Then that massive earthquake happens.

I had to leave work that day because I couldn't stop crying with worry; three of my four kids were in Christchurch. I was so upset – terrified, actually – and I'd had no contact from them. Eventually we spoke on the phone and Niall said she was training on a footy field when the ground just started rolling like a green sea.

John Arthur and Sonny Bill were staying in a hotel and they said it was like a war zone, with fires in the building and the staircase cracked. They ran around making sure people got out. When John Arthur called me on video, I said, 'Is that flames behind you?' He said, 'That's the next-door building on fire.' I so wanted my kids out of there.

Not long after, Sonny Bill was contracted to appear in an ad. Some bigwig in the ad company sent a helicopter to get him from Christchurch.

That day, I get a phone call from Sonny Bill.

'Where are you, Mum?'

'I'm sitting at Nan's having a chat.'

'Go outside,' Sonny Bill says.

So out we go.

'Look up, Mum.'

I looked up and saw a helicopter hovering quite low.

'Can you see me waving?'

He must have asked the pilot to open the door and tip the chopper towards us so we could see him – waving!

'Oh my god! It's Sonny Bill!'

It was such an unexpected bit of humour after the terrible things that happened in the earthquake. He circled a couple of times, waving, then he was off.

I told my friends, and they didn't believe me. Sonny Bill's always been a character, that boy. Has that prankster, joker thing. That's what his family know him best for. – Lee Williams

As far as rugby went, playing with the Crusaders in 2011 made for another great year, though obviously we were all affected by the earthquake. The city was full of broken streets, with thousands of houses destroyed or red-zoned as too dangerous to enter. There's no question we had the Crusader fans in mind every time we ran out onto a field. Playing-wise, it felt I could hardly put a foot wrong. Even when we were up against the tougher South African sides on their home soil – the Stormers, the Cheetahs, the Sharks – me and my Crusader teammates were in the zone, and I was doing crazy offloads, having an absolute ball.

Something else was crazy whenever I played in South Africa. The local fans cheered more for me than their own players. It was embarrassing, actually, and I remember running on with the team for the first time, and Kieran Read looking at me puzzled and smiling. *Am I hearing what I think I am? Is that my name they are chanting?* I guess it was because of the offloads and my particular style of playing; South African players love physicality. And I loved South Africa and its people right back. I even vowed to marry a South African one day – which did actually happen! Cape Town will always hold a special place in my heart because of the hospitality and kindness the locals showed me.

Towards the end of the season, and with the World Cup to come, we eventually succumbed to the fatigue that came from all the long-distance travel to South Africa and Australia, and we lost the final to the Queensland Reds, who had my good mate Quade Cooper playing for them. But it was still a massive year.

I really saw the power of sport during that time, how people depend on their home side to go out and perform for them. With virtually every person in Christchurch affected to some degree by the February earthquake, the city was going through a lot of hardship. The massive clean-up and the start of a long, slow rebuild took its toll, so I think rugby was more important than ever. The people of Christchurch looked forward to us Crusaders playing every week. I've been told many times that we lifted their spirits, especially if we won – and even more so if it was a nail-biting win. Sports fans love the drama, too.

In the days after the quake, I ended up moving into a mate's house because our hotel was deemed unsafe. Johnny and I needed some clothes and it wasn't as if we could go to a menswear store and buy some. The entire city centre was off-limits and suburban shopping malls had been damaged. Niall had been staying with us with her husband, and so together we went into the city to try to get back into our room and retrieve some of our things.

At the time, there was a lot of looting going on. It is a despicable act at any time, but particularly when people's lives have been so devastated. We got to our hotel, and Johnny and I each went to our own apartments. We snuck in and I remember the stairwell and the stairs were all cracked and broken, so that one stair is here while another was over there. Crazy sight. I got into my apartment and gathered up my clothes while my sis kept watch outside.

I heard something and looked out the window and my sister was calling up to me. Cops. Damn. We went down and showed the cops our ID, so they knew we weren't looters, and they recognised me. But they did say they assumed we were up to no good until we explained who we were. It was a weird time.

The only thing that was normal was playing rugby. Although we fell one game short, with everything going on in Christchurch off the field, it was amazing the feats we were achieving on it. Me and the fearsome uso Robbie Fruean were making a lot of noise as a fierce midfield partnership, and a lot of people in the media and the public were calling for higher honours for Robbie. Unknown to many, Robbie had a heart problem from rheumatic fever, something a lot of Islanders have due to poor healthcare growing up. It is just another struggle my community has to face. Despite this, Robbie still managed to carve out a successful career and it is rugby's loss that his heart condition meant he was not able to reach his full fitness potential and play at the highest level. The uso would have looked great in black!

Still, there were games when the old mind starts playing up, letting negative thoughts start dancing around. No-one had any idea of my internal struggles, because I had worked out ways to overcome them by being really physical in a tackle, leading with my shoulder but making it legal by having my arms outstretched, or running hard and often breaking through one or even several defenders. That's how I deal with negativity: try to knock it over!

Like I've said, I approach my sport with a simplistic mindset. Follow a mistake with a positive. A positive with another positive. Reset. Reset. Reset, even when you're stuffed. *Work ethic, Sonny. Work ethic.* And generally, when I kept at it like that, I knew I would play well. If I made a less-than-ferocious tackle, I'd come down hard on myself. *You can do better than that, bro!* None of this two-minded tackle or two-minded carry. Make your mind up and go full-on. All game and every game.

I hope youngsters reading this, or having it read aloud to them, heed what I'm saying. Train better than hard and never let up. Keep it simple and play like every game is your last. You might not get acknowledgement from outsiders straightaway but, more importantly, your teammates will see your efforts. Eventually, you will see the fruits of your labour, maybe not through natural ability but through hard work, discipline and a positive attitude.

—

CHAPTER 8

Pushing the boundaries

So, what about this boxing caper?

Even though I have an exceptional love of playing sport, never in my wildest dreams did I envisage myself a boxer. It came from necessity, to get myself out of debt. Remember, Anthony Mundine and some other close brothers had helped me get myself out of a hole by putting up a million dollars to buy out my contract with the Bulldogs, and I was determined to pay them back as soon as I could.

I was in a bad way at the time: I had walked out on the Bulldogs, and both the club and the NRL were chasing me. I'd gone from having the highest reputation as a player in Australia to being the most hated. I was injured again, and I was a million dollars in debt with no idea how to make that right. They were dark times and desperate times. It was a deep hole and I didn't know how to pull myself out of it. I was doubting myself. Had I made the right decision, leaving the Doggies? Yes – I knew that was one thing I'd done right. If I hadn't walked away, who knows where I would have ended up. I had to go to save myself from myself. If I hadn't found the courage to confront my demons and insecurities, I don't know where I would have ended up, but I know that it wouldn't have been a good place. I thank God that Islam gave me the strength to confront myself. There are a lot of people who never manage to do that and they, and all those around them, suffer.

No-one can change your ways to get yourself out of danger but yourself. It's like smoking or any other addiction: only you can change it. After a year in Toulon learning a new footy code, I was stronger, more focused and looking to secure my financial future, so I was back in Australia learning yet another new sport that might help me do that: boxing.

I spent six weeks in a camp in Brisbane, training, and it turned out to be a really special time in my life. When I came over from France, I was still fighting my demons to some degree; trying to find out who I really was and who I wanted to be. But after six weeks in Brisbane, training, praying and keeping company with Khoder and other knowledgeable Muslim brothers, I could feel the change happening.

One of the Islamic teachings is that to be content with what you have, you have to be in the moment and understand that whatever comes along is a blessing. Even adversity gives us something, teaching us what to be grateful for. Being content with what I have is a life lesson I was finally learning and I was more at peace with myself.

Being in good company and giving my time to charity events made me feel particularly happy, as if one of my yearnings, secret even from myself, had been revealed. I wanted to give back; it just felt so natural and it fitted my empathetic nature. When you're in a good environment with the brothers and all the talk is not about you, the self-centred individual, things become clearer. You can focus on more important things, like gratitude to Allah, understanding moral principles, appreciating nature's beauty.

Allah was constantly on my mind and I was starting to realise that that was why I loved this environment. That's what made it all so special, not the boxing. But the boxing was good too! The first of the seven fights I participated in between 2009 and 2015 knocked a significant sum off my debt. It was 27 May 2009 and I was up against Gary Gurr; he wasn't a boxer, just a bar brawler out for a payday, like me. Jumping in the ring, I was a bit nervous, but as soon as the fight started, my old footy personality kicked in. I was out to dominate. *It's either you or me.* He didn't last long.

When I went back to Toulon, I took with me a stronger commitment to Islam. Moise picked me up from the airport and started to talk about going out to meet girls and I told him I was leaving that life behind. I knew that I wanted to live more for my Creator, wanted to be a better man and a better Muslim. We talked and sounded each other out about our troubles and from then on we both walked that path.

Well, that second year in France turned out to be amazing in terms of growth as a rugby player and, more importantly, growth as a person. It was all thanks to the Islamic faith that I had found my true self. And I'd enjoyed the preparation for that fight with Gurr so much I started to think more about boxing as a sporting challenge.

My second fight took place when I returned to New Zealand in 2010 with the goal of making the All Blacks. I didn't have much prep for that bout, but the guy I was up against couldn't really fight. He lasted two minutes and thirty seconds. Yes, it was a rubbish fight, but at that time, it was more about decreasing my debt than boxing.

In 2011, I had two more fights. The first was back in Australia, against Scott Lewis, who'd knocked out Carl Webb. Webb was a former Australian Golden gloves champ and rugby league enforcer turned boxer who was very good at both sports – till Lewis surprised everyone and knocked him out. Webb got fatigued, which in any sport invites danger, but in boxing the consequences are lights out. It's a cruel sport. For me, it was the same old story in the ring. I went from really nervous and uncertain to achieving something special purely from hard work and determination. I wasn't a boxer – far from it – but that didn't stop me from getting in there and having a go.

For my first four fights, I'd been my own trainer. I didn't know any technique, didn't know anything. I just relied on my athlete's instincts to move around and throw jabs. That can only take you so far, as I found out against Lewis. That fight went the whole six rounds and I won on points but I realised if I wanted to step up and fight better opponents, my approach would have to change.

In Australia, I reached out to Anthony's dad, Tony Mundine. Tony was a former British Commonwealth middleweight champion who everyone thought might go all the way to world champion. But then he went up against undisputed world champion Carlos Monzón of Argentina, and he got beaten. Interestingly, Monzón's life ended in tragedy: he was sentenced to eleven years in prison for killing his partner and then was killed in a car crash while on weekend furlough leave. Life lessons like that remind us all that triumph can go hand in hand with disaster.

The fifth fight was the one I held to raise money for the Christchurch Earthquake Appeal, and it gave me the same feeling I'd had when involved in charity events back in Brisbane.

My next chance to box came after the 2011 Rugby World Cup win: a win the country had waited twenty-four years for. We played in front of 60,000 people at home – it was awesome to be part of rugby union history and an unforgettable climax to a really good year. I'd been a part of the Canterbury ITM-winning team, played a part in the Crusader Super Rugby grand final. Now I was a World Cup winner with the All Blacks. I definitely surpassed all my own personal expectations in that first year back home in New Zealand. As a rookie rugby player in the fiercest, most competitive rugby environment in the world, I was holding my own and then some. What a year!

Then, in February 2012, I had a chance to win the New Zealand boxing heavyweight title. I used my training for this fight as a way of getting fit for my first season with the Chiefs in the Super Rugby competition. I'm thinking how cool it would be to look back at my sporting career and have New Zealand heavyweight boxing champion listed among my accomplishments. Of course, making my family proud was another goal for me, because my grandad had fought for the New Zealand cruiserweight title and lost.

I was originally slated to go up against Richard Tutaki, but he ran into some troubles, so US-born, New Zealand-based Clarence Tillman III stood up instead. We asked Tillman why he wanted to fight me; he would have seen my last fights and thought, *Who is this mug? He can't fight, this guy's a joke – a dual-code rugby player right out of his league.* He disrespected me from the start. I can understand where he was coming from, thinking I'd had only four fights against easybeats, none of them real boxers. He was probably saying to himself: *Guy can't even throw a proper punch.* And he was right: I didn't really know how to throw a punch. But Allah has blessed me to be a fast learner when it comes to sport. I had my first actual professional boxing camp and I was sparring with good boxers and holding my own. I improved so much over those twelve weeks. Yes, I had Mount Everest to climb because of my inexperience, but I was feeling better about myself every day. Training is my forte and, man, did I train for this fight.

By the eighth week, I had sparred eleven to twelve rounds with four different boxers, one of them former world champion and my good mate Anthony Mundine. I held my own against all of them. I had the mindset, and it was about dedication, just waking up every day and getting into my regime without let-up. On the pads with Tony, I felt comfortable for the first time, like I belonged there; slip, catch, feint.

After a gruelling eight weeks in Sydney, I had four more weeks in Hamilton. I was really, really fit, though still had a bit to learn technique-wise. My main sparring partner in New Zealand was young Joseph Parker. He hadn't turned professional yet, but the quality was there. You learn so much from sparring, especially with someone like Parker. I had some good sessions with him, copped some good punches and gave a few of my own back. Sparring is the next best thing to the actual fight. Watching back the videos of my sparring with Joseph, a future heavyweight champ, even I was surprised by how much progress I'd made. I guess being Pop's grandson meant fighting was always in my genes.

My fight with Tillman started before the first bell was even rung, with my opponent shoving then punching me at the weigh-in – a punch I felt. Walking in for our weigh-in and press conference, you could feel the atmosphere; it was almost like Tillman hated me, and for no good reason other than contempt, I guess, for my daring to hop into the ring with him, an African American guy from New Orleans. Boxing is a gladiator sport and it attracts all types.

As soon as we rocked in, Tillman locked eyes with me. Yet I was looking at him thinking he wasn't so huge after all. He started the trash talk, like he was disgusted at being in the same ring as me. I'm feeling confident because of all the work I've done. I'd fought good fighters and held my own. So, I had nothing to be scared about. We go face to face and he really starts mouthing off. And I transform into the man I am on the footy field: I stand my ground.

I'm giving some lip back, then he shoved me and king-hit me with a hook. But even though I was a little rattled, I was that fit that I thought he had just pushed me. My boys went off. My brother tried to get to Tillman, Liam Messam piled in, Choc, old Tony, they were all trying to get a shot in. Because you don't do what Tillman did.

The media narrative was that it was just another Sonny Bill circus. Watching the video, I saw he really hooked me a beauty. I'm a little bit rocked by this, naturally, because I know the real-deal punches are coming soon. I have to admit, I later went to my room and lay down thinking about how hard that guy punched. Lay there looking at the ceiling thinking, *If he rocked me with that punch, what's going to happen in the fight?*

The next day was fight day. Tana Umaga came to my house before the fight, and I remember the look on his face, like he was really worried for me. Gave me a kiss on the head and said, 'Good luck, Uso.' From that look, I realised everyone must have thought I was going to get smashed.

So, I rock up to the stadium and I'm pretty nervous. In the ring, Tillman's walking towards me, trying to stare me down. Immediately, my old self steps up. That white

Sāmoan kid the big Islanders tried to bully and smash, to step over. It was just like that, having that moment to think, *You think you're going to put it on me? All right, let's see what you've got.*

The first-round bell goes and I'm moving, trying to get a feel for it, and I feel like I'm faster than him. I throw once at the body, then he comes in and tries to throw, but they're wild punches and I evade them easily. I throw a hook that just misses him.

I step back and then I hear Choc: 'Check hook, Sonny! Check hook!' His favourite move, where he pretends to throw a jab and then throws a hook. You have those little moments in the ring where you can hear the voice of someone you know. I threw a hard jab, another to the body, before I went into that pretend jab then threw the hook. Bam! Right on the button.

Tillman stumbled around and I went into jungle mode, like I was having a fight at school. No technique, I just started swinging. Next thing, the ref, Lance Revill, stops the fight. I've won! I'm the New Zealand national heavyweight champion! To this day, it was one of the best feelings of any sporting event in my life – I think because of where I came from, with no boxing experience, the stuff I'd been through. And here I am, the official heavyweight boxing champion of New Zealand. Yeah, it was some buzz.

My next biggie, my sixth fight, was a year later, in February 2013, against South African heavyweight Francois Botha. He'd fought heavyweight legends Evander Holyfield, Mike Tyson, Lennox Lewis, and the tough-as-teak Shannon Briggs. Sure, Botha was in his forties when we fought, but he came with forty-eight wins, eight losses, three draws.

I was playing rugby in Japan, doing boxing training as well. I did my pec in a game, tore it. I was out for ten weeks and I thought we'd have to call the fight off. Our date was already set but I needed an operation. I talked about it with Khoder and I decided, *Yeah, this is an old guy, I only need three weeks' training.* But in the back of my mind I was thinking about the greats he'd fought. Still, I told myself I'd be able to move and dance and tire the old guy out. I flew a physio over from Australia to work on my pec day and night, and then we only had two and a half weeks before the fight. Sure, I had the injury, but I was in pretty good condition otherwise and thought I'd just dance for the ten rounds.

Fight night comes around before you know it. I'm looking across at my opponent, who has fought all these top names; okay, he didn't beat any, but he was no pushover either.

The first round went well. The second, even better; I was finding my target. But when I sat down at the end of round two, I felt buggered. And there was Botha, ignoring his stool, standing up. I knew then it was gonna be a long night. He got some good shots in and in the last minute of the ninth he landed a punch that shook me. I don't remember much about the details because of the concussion I carried after but the controversy around the length of the fight is hard to forget. But that fight was always going to be ten rounds, though others started saying it was cut short. It is easy to watch the replay on YouTube. In my corner at the end of the second round, I either spat or took out my mouthguard. My corner was talking, but I wasn't listening. I looked at my brother, Johnny, and he was looking at me with this real scared expression. His face was saying to me, *I know you're gassed. Your bro knows you better than anyone.* And I looked at him and did a silent, *Yeah.*

Yet I went out and fought Botha, and even though I remember feeling gassed, it doesn't look like that in the replay. All I know is, fitness and prep are everything, and my two and a half weeks of prep was not enough. It was my core fitness that got me there.

In those last four minutes, starting when Botha clipped me in the ninth with a minute to go, inner nature, animal instincts, took over. I just had to hang on, survive the onslaught. I don't remember those two little flurries in the last. I was in the survival zone.

Training with Tony Mundine, he doesn't really do the technical; his objective is to work on fitness first, then the best teacher: sparring. In preparing for Botha, I did no sparring, so it was a mad learning experience both for myself – to do sparring for real – and learning the sport. It ain't play. It's coming up against a full-grown hulky man of vast experience who's intent on knocking you out. Like any heavyweight, when he connects, you feel it down to your toes. Other than a gunfight, this is the ultimate arena.

It was a learning experience for Khoder, too, in seeing that fitness allowed me to box those ten rounds, moving around, firing off shots. Learning that few sports are as deadly serious, carrying potentially terrible consequences if you drop your guard, lose concentration for a second or two. With a guy like this, a mistake means lights out.

It was a close call for me because Botha took me to a place of fatigue I had never experienced before. In hindsight, as a novice fighting ten rounds with only three weeks' prep, I am proud I was able to hang on and win that match-up. From a technical point of view, Botha covered my jab by coming over it. I didn't really know what he was doing. I didn't have that repetition learning in my head: jab, feint, jab, move to your left and throw the right cross, next step in and throw the left hook, whatever. I was just going by instinct. I won that one, but it could have gone either way. I took away the title and a concussion.

I only had one more fight, against Chauncy Welliver in 2015, the year of the Rugby World Cup. I prepped really well, and the eight-round fight reflected that: I won easily.

Now that I've retired from footy, I have decided to dedicate my final last sporting flourish to boxing. Boxing is a way to transition out of sport. Though maybe I'll do some coaching of either footy code. The fighter of now is not the same one who fought Botha. There is so much growth left to do, so much learning, it makes each day exciting because of the challenge. It's that mad training mindset again.

But boxing is a tough sport. You are always one moment away from disaster, and you are completely on your own with no teammates to support you and back you up. The struggle I have in getting better as a boxer and learning more about what works and what doesn't is that I can't just fight anonymously to get experience. I don't have the luxury of making mistakes without anyone watching and analysing. But the challenge to overcome fear, to become a better fighter, drives me. It is always the challenge that pushes me forwards. Overcoming fear. Going into an uncomfortable situation. That takes courage.

Now I'm out of league and rugby union and have taken on being a television rugby union and rugby league commentator, I'm as uncomfortable as I've ever been. But I am doing it. I am driven by that desire to be better at something. And also, to stand up as a man of colour and be broadcast into lounge rooms around the country, that is a huge deal. That is something bigger than me, so despite my fear, I am taking that opportunity. If I took the soft option, I would never have come back to New Zealand after Toulon. I could have stayed there and played for France. The money they pay the top players in France is really good. But I wouldn't have been true to myself. I wanted to be an All Black.

And look how it turned out: I played fifty-eight Tests for the All Blacks, won a lot of respect and even won over some of my detractors.

Taking yourself right out of your comfort zone pays big dividends, and not just in overcoming the challenge. For too long I was also fighting my low self-esteem. Truth is, I still am. Being live on television? Me, the shy Sāmoan boy who knows he'll never defeat all his demons?

Yes. Me, the half-caste Sāmoan – take out shy; it doesn't matter if I'm shy or not. Me, the league and union player, on the small screen, speaking to an audience around the world. That's what I mean.

I would love it if every brown-skinned youngster – if youngsters of any ethnic origin – heeded these words and said to themselves: *If Sonny Bill can do it, then so can I.*

Kids, if you already have doubts in your mind, or demons you wrestle with each and every day, please be gentle with yourself. But also understand that you are not alone in that. So many of us carry internal struggles that no-one can see. We all have deficiencies, no-one is perfect. Believe me about that. In my time as a sportsman, I have learned that even the people I've admired and thought had it all figured out have their struggles. No matter who you are or how strong someone may appear, everyone has difficulties they need to overcome. No-one is perfect. If I could, I'd put my arm over all of your shoulders and let you know, yes, life might be a struggle sometimes, but with discipline, hard work and patience you can make it better. You might have to learn to live with your inner demons like I have, but you will make it. So don't give up on it. Things can always get better.

I was talking with a young athlete recently who wanted advice. I told him he needed to sacrifice if he really wanted to succeed. You can't lose yourself in social media. You can't watch TV or chill on your phone all day and expect to make progress. Training or doing something positive – rather than wasting your time, and your life, staring at a screen – is the only way to make things happen. It is up to you to define what you want and then work for it. I have always had that focused work ethic but now the daily structure and discipline that Islam has given me has sharpened that.

It has allowed me to stay on top of my demons for the most part; praying five times a day, for example, allows me to step back every day and see the big picture. It gives me the headspace to reflect and to be grateful for the things in life that matter to me – my children, my loving wife, my loving family, my beautiful house with fancy wallpaper. In a world that is so fast-paced and that puts too much value on fleeting things that only gratify for the briefest of times, it's easy to get lost and caught up in valuing things of no substance. I did that and I am very proud that my faith helped me refocus on what truly matters. I found the peace I was searching for, and it has allowed me to thrive in all areas of life, especially mentally, taught me the importance of gratitude and to follow an empathic heart. So whatever path you end up on, it needs to be one that gives you a positive attitude and a driven mindset because a kid with this is a kid who's going places.

I need to stress that I can still get negative thoughts saying, *You're worthless. Who do you think you are to go and commentate? Who are you to have your own gym with the aim of going as far as you can in boxing?* Even those close to me don't get why I feel like this. To be honest, sometimes I don't. But it's a daily struggle. For all my achievements, for all the praise, the acclaim, the million compliments, I know I'm in for a daily fight with my biggest opponent: myself.

CHAPTER 9

Insha Allah
(God willing)

Faith is an intimate connection between a person and their Creator and for me, faith has brought great comfort and self-knowledge. I realise that the One God doesn't need me at all but I, on the other hand, can't live without the One God. One of the reasons I connect with Islam so strongly is because I believe faith should put you on a path to be the best version of yourself and Islam has definitely done this for me. With my faith, I believe in the afterlife and that when I die I will end up in Jannah (paradise) or Jahannam (hellfire), depending on my actions in this dunya (world). My belief in the One God makes me accountable and I strive constantly to better myself. I know that Allah sees all that I do and more importantly what is in my heart, that knowledge and the discipline of Islam helps focus me to keep myself on the straight path daily. I have learned that a life with no boundaries is one I get lost in. The Prophet Muhammad (Peace Be Upon Him) said there will come a time when holding onto your religion will be like holding onto a hot coal. I strive to hold that hot coal daily. I have also learned that the best Muslim is the one who has the best character, someone who keeps the Oneness of God at the front of their mind, while being well-mannered and respectful of family and the wider community. Someone who is honest, kind and shows courage when needing to speak up for the voiceless and fight against injustice will reach Paradise. This is what I strive to do. It strengthens my faith in Allah to know that unjust, corrupt and inhumane people will have to answer to the Knower of All one day. To be honest, I don't even wish to entertain the thought of hell for one second. May the Most High keep me and those I love away from hellfire.

Islam is a way of life and it is obligatory for a Muslim to strive to pray five times a day, give to charity, fast, visit the sick and think about the less fortunate. It is a religion based on five pillars of belief and practice:

Shahada (faith)

Muslims believe the only God is Allah and that the Prophet Muhammad (Peace Be Upon Him) is the final messenger of God.

194

Salat (prayer)

Islam suggests worship five times a day: at Fajr (dawn), Dhuhr (noon), Asr (late afternoon), Maghrib (sunset) and Isha (night). A person must wash (hands, mouth, nose, face, arms and feet) before prayer, but if you can't, you can still pray. You can pray alone or in a congregation at the masjid, where you get the most reward. For me, the beauty of praying five times a day is that it gives me a connection with my Creator all throughout the business of the day. It protects me against temptations and keeps me focused on what is important for me in this life, my family, my wife and being a good man, so it gives me a contentment in my heart. Jumah (Friday noon prayer) is special to Muslims and is done in a masjid if possible. Muslims face in the direction of Mecca, in Saudi Arabia, when they pray. In eastern Australia, that means facing in an easterly direction and in New Zealand in a south-westerly direction.

Zakat (alms)

Islam requires that charity, known as zakat, be given to the poor or needy. In addition to this, Muslims are encouraged to give as much as they can in voluntary charity. (This is not just monetary; it can be volunteering or other acts of kindness and generosity.) You don't have to give if you have nothing to give. Islam directs you to look after those close to you – your family, your friends. It encourages you to help those in your inner circle who need it first.

Sawm (fasting)

During the month of Ramadan, the ninth month of the lunar calendar, Muslims fast from dawn to sunset and gather in the evenings to break their fast. While fasting, Muslims are required to abstain from food and drink, including water. But the fast goes beyond this; you are also required to abstain from sex and you must strive for purity of thought. Muslims are required to start fasting when they reach puberty, although some younger children may want to fast and they are permitted to do this. My eldest daughter, Imaan, did a few days of fasting with me this year. It was a beautiful thing to eat our Surhur, a meal before first prayer at sunrise, with her. I was so grateful to sit with her to eat our porridge and in the calm and peace of those moments I felt such a deep connection to Allah and to my daughter. Eid al-Fitr is one of the major holidays in Islam and is a three-day celebration marking the end of the Ramadan fast. The date is determined by the sight of the new moon. Eid is a celebration that includes family gatherings, prayers, feasts and gift-giving. One of the most beneficial things you can do for your body is to intermittently fast. Not only does that month of fasting benefit me physically but I can feel the benefits mentally as well. It always seems to humble me and give me gratitude for the simple things, like being able to eat and drink. Ramadan always seems to come at just the right time for me.

Hajj (pilgrimage)

Every Muslim is required to make the pilgrimage to Mecca once in their life if they are financially and physically able to do so. All outward symbols of rank and wealth are erased during the pilgrimage, as Muslims from every part of the globe come together for the purpose of worshipping God. Muslims who have made the pilgrimage are referred to as hajji and are celebrated and respected when they get home. I have visited Mecca on an umrah pilgrimage, which means visiting at a time of the year other than during the hajj. It was an awesome experience to pay respect, strengthen my faith, pray and learn. Though I have done umrah myself, I can't wait to perform the hajj with my family. Insha Allah, soon.

* * *

For me, Islam has lit the way through the darkness. It's given me a sense of empowerment of the deepest kind. It gave me the strength to turn away from self-indulgence and the world of alcohol, drugs and superficial relationships, and I can honestly say that without that strength I would have been lost. Islam has bettered every part of my life. I know without question Islam has made me happy, content and given me solace. But with Islam, as with everything in life worth doing, discipline is all-important. You have to commit. I did.

That discipline has given me a freedom to go wherever I want in life. It has helped to heal the unsure, shy and self-conscious young man I was and enabled me to strive to be better all the time.

Discipline and prayer have given me natural highs that no amount of alcohol or drugs could ever give. Those things might feel good at the time, but the day after, the week after, you feel something toxic inside you. In Islam, we get up early to perform our first prayer of the day. I then usually read some of the Quran and then wake up my wife, trying not to wake up one or two of the kids, who have often snuck into our bed in the night. It's such a beautiful beginning to the day because your heart knows you've started the morning doing the right thing.

For me, the beauty of these prayers is like protection against a world that is all about being on the go and accumulating. Being able to step back and see the big picture and be grateful for what I have been blessed with is an important thing.

I think Islam has helped me to understand that rather than accumulating material things, one should accumulate values; it has given me a moral code to live by. Simple things like giving your time visiting the sick or helping a charity out is another form of zakat. I challenge anyone to go see a kid with cancer or to witness an adult suffering terrible pain, and not feel grateful for your own good health.

Yes, I can still get caught up in the worldly rat-race and put value on things that in the long run won't bring me the happiness my soul yearns for. But that doesn't happen so much anymore now I have grown and learned so much from the teachings of the Prophet Muhammad (Peace Be Upon Him) and from reading the holy Quran. If I do have moments of discontent, I know how to get back on track. Having a content and happy heart is one of the most precious things you can strive for. This is how my soul loves to feel. I've been lucky to achieve a lot but what means the most is to have reached a point in my life where I feel content and happy. To me, this is a small slice of what paradise must feel like. I am so grateful to Allah for the blessings I have.

I say his faith is the most important thing to happen to Sonny Bill. Finding something he believed in so much, that changed his mental attitude. As his mother, I knew he had a special goodness from a young age. The kid who saved his pretty skinny pocket money to buy his mum fudge? What kid even thinks of that?

Sonny Bill cares deeply about others and he'll stick up for people being treated badly, no matter the consequences to himself. He has compassion and empathy, qualities you don't often find in exceptional sportspeople, as they're usually so focused they zone others out.

Sonny Bill has gone from being a boy of few words to a good talker. When he's explaining his religion, he does it in such clear terms that even I can understand. He's so honest in what he says and talks from the heart. Yes, he's definitely got better at talking as he's got older and had more and more diverse experiences. Actually, I feel so blessed that all my four kids are good people.

I've become a Muslim too. I follow the basic things, like being good to people, helping others, being careful what you say about others so you don't hurt their feelings. The lessons of Islam are about being a good person, just like my mum taught me. – Lee Williams

Like so many people, I was horrified when I heard the news of what happened in Christchurch in March 2019. Even now, I struggle to put into words how deeply this affected me. The horrific attack on two Christchurch mosques, when fifty-one worshippers were killed and over forty injured at Friday prayers, devastated those communities and horrified people right around the world. That vile

Alana and I with our little blessings. God willing, we are blessed with more one day.

Some of my All Blacks teammates in Paris.

With Springboks captain Siya Kolisi, South Africa's first black captain.

A Kiwi and an Englishman: always a battle, always respect, no matter what the code.

The final siren – me and Jerome Kaino celebrating the 2011 World Cup victory.

Offloading to Nehe Milner-Skudder in the 2015 World Cup final.

Showing support to Jesse Kriel after the All Blacks defeated South Africa in the 2015 World Cup semi-final.

Winners! Me and Ma'a Nonu with the Rugby World Cup.

I always tried to play with passion and physicality, especially at the highest level. But sometimes you get it wrong, as I did on this night. I became only the second All Blacks player in history to be red carded. It was a big game versus the Lions in 2017, and it was tough knowing I had let my teammates down.

With Charlie Line – he is wearing my medal.

A special night playing for the Auckland Blues, with Tana Umaga as coach. Here I am offloading to Ihaia West for the match-winner against the Lions at Eden Park in 2017.

Ofa Tu'ungafasi and I giving thanks during the 2019 Rugby World Cup.

Sevens rugby was fast – this photo is from the 2016 Wellington tournament.

Niall, Mum and me.

With the great Usain Bolt.

It was time for a new challenge and a new dream – representing my country at the 2016 Rio Olympics in the rugby sevens. I was so proud that I made that team and so did my sister Niall. My dream was shattered by injury but Niall brought a medal home.

In Christchurch, alongside some of the Pacific region's most well-known Muslim athletes – Hazem El Masri, Ofa Tu'ungafasi, Willis Meehan and Bachar Houli – who came to give support and respect to the brothers and sisters who had been shot in the horrific attacks.

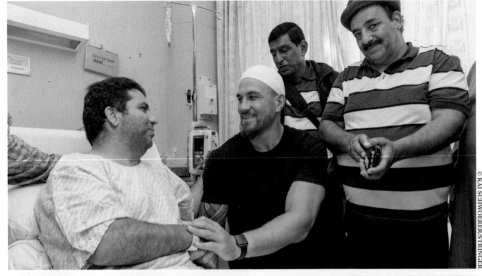

© KAI SCHWOERER/STRINGER

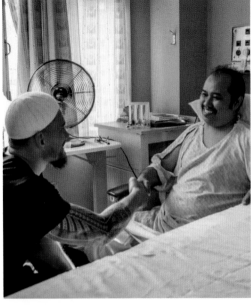

In Lebanon visiting a Syrian refugee camp.

The 2011 and 2015 victorious All Blacks World Cup teams. Grateful to have worn the jersey fifty-eight times and to have shared some special memories with some good men. Always Alhamdulillah.

The end of my time with the All Blacks. Standing alongside these men was an honour: Ben Smith, Ryan Crotty, Kieran Read and Matt Todd.

If my story shows anything, it is that hard work and focus can make a difference. I hope I can encourage others to back themselves and be brave enough to chase their dreams. What matters most to me now is faith, family, friends and helping to point out injustice in the world. I have been given a gift and a profile, and I have to use them to make a difference. And I still love my sport! Rugby union, rugby league, rugby sevens, boxing – love them all.

act showed me that good people will always support one another and that bad and evil exists and we should always speak out against that. Later, I found out that the murderer had also scoped out mosques in Ponsonby and Hamilton. My daughter and I often go to mosque together after I pick her up from school on a Friday and we could just as easily have been caught up in this murderous rampage.

It is at times like this that fame can help make things a little easier for people or provide comfort. A lot of my Muslim brothers and sisters reached out to see what they could do to help. Anthony Mundine, Hazem El Masri, Bachar Houli and Ofa Tu'ungafasi are just some who came together to visit Christchurch and to speak with those who'd been injured and those who had lost loved ones. That is a strong message in Islam, to look out for each other. Fighting against racism and hate speech was an important thing for me to do after what happened and I will continue to support my brothers and sisters who have been affected by those murders.

I owe a lot to my Islamic faith and I will always try to give back when I can.

* * *

One of the first players to fly the Muslim flag in the NRL was Anthony Mundine, who made his first-grade debut in 1993 for the St George Dragons. Another player proud of his Islamic faith is Hazem El Masri, a Bulldogs player who made his first-grade debut in 1996 and who I played with at the club. Hazem represented New South Wales and Australia, and was one of the best kickers in the game. Choc and Hazem are both incredible sportsmen and very good men, and I admire them both.

When you look at it from a pure sporting perspective, Choc's career is really amazing and almost second to none. He is definitely one of the best sportsmen to ever come out of Australia. He was at the height of his sporting powers when he switched from footy to boxing, following in the footsteps of his legendary old man (and my current boxing trainer) Tony, who my children know as Uncle Cowboy. Choc would then dominate boxing for many years in Australia and go on to become a three-time world champion. Choc's sporting talent in rugby league and boxing is often overshadowed because he is outspoken in his personal views, especially for his people. He can rub some up the wrong way and sections of the media have been harsh, but to me he will always be a man with a loving heart who passionately speaks up for what he believes in. When I was at my lowest ebb, he was there to help me, both financially and spiritually. I will forever be grateful.

Hazem and I were close at the Dogs and although we never spoke of faith back then, I always respected the way he carried himself. At the time, I was blind to that type of faith as my religion then was the game of rugby league. One of the regrets I have about when I left the Bulldogs was the fact I didn't show our friendship more respect and tell Hazem how I was struggling and why I was leaving the game. The boy I was back then didn't have the words, but I know Hazem was hurt and took it personally that I didn't speak to him about it all. With my head in turmoil, that just wasn't on my radar, but the beauty of Islam is that we are taught to forgive one another. I'm glad that we have become close again over the years.

When I played footy with Hazem, I had no understanding of what Ramadan meant for an elite athlete. But the one thing I am sure all Muslim athletes get asked about is how they combine training and playing with fasting during Ramadan. I often get questions about how it impacts on my training and how I play in a game.

As I said earlier, Ramadan is a very special time and part of my connection with my Creator. It is about focusing on being grateful for the things we have and concentrating on being a better person, so it is a time I look forward to. But the first week of fasting can mean your energy flags, until you start to get used to it, so Muslim athletes have to modify some of what they do. When it comes to the mechanics of training, I find fasting easiest with footy-based training, and so I push back any weight training until I break the fast at night.

When I first started fasting, I was very scientific about the process. I'd work out when I should eat carbs and what other types of food would help. But the whole fasting and playing sport is not an issue when you believe in what you are doing and are committed to it. More recently, I have stopped trying to manage it all so tightly and just trust the process.

Islam has helped me in so many ways and embracing all the pillars of Islam is important to me.

CHAPTER 10

You do better when you know better

What a special year 2013 would be, not only for what Allah allowed me to achieve on the field but, even more so, for what happened off it.

While I was playing Super Rugby for the Chiefs in 2012, these guys from the Panasonic Wild Knights flew over from Japan to offer me a rugby contract. I told them I had already committed to going back to league and playing for the Sydney Roosters and I couldn't break my word. I had made that commitment to Roosters Chairman Nick Politis years before. But these guys were really keen to have me, so their offer went from a minimum twelve-month deal to a twelve-game, four-month offer. I appreciated the respect they showed, flying all the way over to New Zealand just to talk for a couple of hours, and I liked their enthusiasm and the challenge their offer presented me, so after clearing it with the Roosters, I said yes.

I arrived in Japan in August 2012, right after winning the Bledisloe Cup with the All Blacks, and put my head down learning the plays so I could give my all to the team. I made my debut in round two of the competition. We narrowly lost that game, but I played the full eighty minutes and felt good. The next week we won, and I was getting a feel for the Japanese rugby ways. But it all fell apart in round eight, when I was injured. I left the field and went straight to the hospital for an MRI scan. At first it didn't seem too bad, but further tests showed a serious pectoral tear which required an operation, and that meant I would need time to recover. I was disappointed I couldn't be there for my Wild Knights teammates and help them reach the heights they aspired to, and for the Panasonic fans, who showed me a lot of faith and love. Although where we were living wasn't known as a tourist destination, I loved my time playing in the Japanese comp. The fast pace and high level of skill the Japanese play with was a surprise but I can see why the Cherry Blossoms are pushing some of the top teams in the world these days.

It was a daunting time as I had to have an operation, have the scheduled fight against Francois Botha and be fit to start with the Sydney Roosters for the 2013 NRL season, so there was a lot of pressure. But the truth was, I was getting used to that. And now I had Allah in my corner I could deal with that pressure head-on. But I was about to find out that 2013 had more in store for me than I had ever imagined.

* * *

I was shopping in the city, in Sydney, and that day I spotted the woman who would become my future wife, working in a clothing store. I was with Johnny, and I don't know what gave me the bravado – my wife would tell you it was her beauty, so let's go with that. I saw this beautiful woman and so asked Johnny to look at some clothes and I walked up to her and started chatting. Her name was Alana and after we'd talked for a while, I asked for her phone number and said I wanted to take her out to dinner.

She declined and wouldn't give me her number – in fact, she asked how many other women I'd approached that day. The audacity! This was a woman who wasn't afraid to stand up for herself or call me out, and I guess that only made me want to get to know her more. Later, I found out Alana had South African heritage and that South African fire was on display to me immediately. (That fire is something I see nowadays in our children, especially little Aisha. I can picture her now with her arms folded, her face with her eyebrows in a bunch telling me off. Alhamdulillah, the blessings of children. Insha Allah, that fire is only used by my kids positively when they get older or I am in trouble.)

I left my phone number with Alana's colleague and I didn't hear anything for a couple of weeks. Then she finally messaged me and we talked. Alana told me that she knew I was a footy player and had been wary. Understandable, when you consider my past reputation. We talked for a while and she explained that she'd talked to her cousins, who told her I was now a Muslim, and that that was the reason she had decided to meet me, but she didn't tell me she was Muslim herself.

After we chatted, we arranged to meet up where Alana was living, at her aunty's house. On the way, I stopped at a service station to get petrol and texted to ask if she wanted anything. Her message came back: 'Yes, please. Eight ice creams.' *Eight? Damn, that is one sweet tooth,* I remember thinking. I bought eight ice creams and rocked up to the address Alana had given me.

A man, who was her uncle, answered the door and he greeted me in the Muslim way: 'Assalamu alaikum.' I was invited inside and in the hallway there was all this Quranic writing and Islamic art on the walls and then there was her family, who the eight ice creams were for. Before that,

I'd had no idea that Alana was Muslim. Obviously family meant a lot to her and I had a good chat with them all, and then Alana and I spoke for about an hour. Our shared faith and other shared interests got me wanting a stronger connection with her. I left there knowing this was a sign from my Creator. I wasn't partying or even drinking at the time, and was definitely not living that toxic lifestyle I had been the last time I played NRL but nor was I in a place where I could say I was at complete peace with my Creator.

Driving home, I gave myself a real hard inner talking-to. I was living back in Sydney, playing for the Roosters, and I admit it would have been so easy to slip back into the bad behaviour that had got me in trouble in the past. But I didn't want that; I knew I had been blessed with so much, and I didn't want to go back to those dark days. I had to be a better Muslim, and I just had a feeling Alana was key to that. I told myself my meeting Alana was a sign. It was time for me to really be a man. Time to stop being selfish and time to step closer to Allah.

* * *

I was halfway through the season with the Roosters. When I joined in 2013, they were near the bottom of the ladder. But now we were being talked about as potential finalists and I was playing really good footy. It was a big decision to come back to the NRL because I was aware that one day I would come up against my old Bulldogs teammates and I knew some of them and some of the fans did not think of me kindly. There was still a lot of anger at me because of what had happened. But I was not the young man they used to know; I didn't drink, and there'd be no more raucous pub and club sessions. I had made peace with myself and my past behaviour.

It didn't feel like I'd been away from the game for five years. I guess muscle memory kicked back in. I was living in the fancy Eastern Suburbs and Alana's first impression of me was right: I had been seeing a few girls casually, which I knew as a Muslim was wrong. Yet none of them were touching my soul. I say that without wanting to be disrespectful to these women at all. The issue was with myself, about who and what I truly wanted to be and what I wanted in my life. To any young man involved in sport at a high level, the dream is supposed to be what I had on a silver – or gold – platter. But it wasn't making me happy. I felt lonely and disconnected. I truly believe that without boundaries in your life you will eventually follow only your own desires and it will lead you into poor decisions and selfish behaviour. I may have changed many of my ways but I was still selfish in my desires when it came to the biggest test of all – women. May Allah forgive me.

Alana was beautiful, but she was different from the other girls I knew. Not so conscious of my image. When we talked, I felt like it meant something. When her uncle opened her door that day and greeted me, it was a reminder of where I needed to be, of where my mind should be – a reminder that this wasn't just another woman I was chasing. I knew I had to step up and be better.

The day after seeing Alana and meeting her family, I changed my phone number and deleted my contacts. Four weeks later, we were married. Eight years later, we have four little blessings in our life. Some would say, that's crazy, there is no way you could possibly get it right in four weeks. I say to them, I married my beautiful fiery wife for Allah's sake and not only has she helped me become a better version of myself, we have been blessed with so much happiness and four children also.

> When I met Sonny, it so happened that we were at the same point of wanting more spiritual meaning in our lives. We met at the right time and grew together and kind of learned along the way. And though we had our moments, we stuck with it and came to a point of strength because we'd started at the same sort of uncertain place. – Alana Williams

Islamic courtship is very different from what others may experience. When Alana said yes to me, that was the start of our journey together. We both wanted to grow. I wanted to keep being a better person. Faith, family, my wife are what matters to me. To be honest, when we first got married, I know we didn't love each other, but we definitely respected each other and we knew if we worked at it and valued each other, love would come. We always strive to be the best person we can be for each other.

We are learning. We've definitely had our fair share of arguments and the last thing I want to paint is a picture-perfect household, because it definitely isn't that. With time, patience, effort, understanding, respect and connection to Allah, I can humbly say we are in a great place together. As Muslims, we believe that marriage is half your religion because of the protection it gives you. It protects you from temptation, and you focus instead on the relationship with your husband or wife, and the close friendship that grows between you.

I love my wife and appreciate all she does for myself and our children. I guess, like life, marriage is a work in progress. I'd say the key for us as a couple has been the growth, whether that be in improving our knowledge of Islam or just understanding each other better. I think any family juggling four kids and the demands of life knows that the struggles are constant, they never stop. But there are also very happy times.

Alana and I both want the same things for our children. We want our house to be a peaceful place and to bring our children up to have strong morals and ethics and also to give them the confidence and strength to be proud of who they are. I don't want them ever to be afraid to voice their opinion or speak up for themselves. It is scary because we live in an age where there are often no healthy boundaries. The rates of addiction to alcohol, drugs and gambling are high. Suicide is an issue in our young and depression and anxiety are growing diseases. I know from my experiences in my late teens and early twenties, I could have ended up in a much darker place. I know people I mixed with back then are still struggling and fighting with their demons. Alana and I will do everything we can to help keep our children from having negative experiences like that. With Allah helping us, we will guide them and protect them and I will pray that my Creator helps keep my children and my wife safe always.

It's the old story: you do better when you know better. I know so much better now. I thank Allah for all of it.

* * *

By 2013, I knew a lot better but the decision to come back to Sydney and play for the Roosters meant I would again have to confront the demons that had seen me leave the Bulldogs almost five years before. And it also meant I could make peace with my leaving once and for all with most of my former teammates. I was happy to see many of them personally and talk through what had happened. I had coffee with the old skipper Andrew Ryan and it was good to chat to him and others. I was able to convey that I was grateful for the opportunities that the Bulldogs had given me and I now had the confidence to face this situation and move forwards in life without any animosity or any ill feelings around the club.

My relationship with the Canterbury fans was more complicated. Many of them were very generous and whenever I ran into them in the street they were always quick to remind me that although they were Dogs fans and had been upset when I'd left the club, they still supported me. I felt good talking to them and always walked away feeling better. But then there were others who would never let me forget that I walked out on the Dogs. They were still angry and didn't think that the NRL should have let me back into the game or that Nick Politis should ever have been allowed to sign me up. Players, coaches and board members leave clubs all the time, some by choice and others not. The business of elite sport is brutal but the loyalties of many still hark back to the spirit of club rugby, something I understood. These fans fuelled their anger by hurling abuse at me and saying the most hideous things about me and my family, yelling from the sidelines when I was on the field and occasionally saying things in public. Some of this was hard to cop, but I realised to still feel this strongly they must have, at one time, felt a lot of admiration for me and felt let down. I'll say to these fans, Canterbury Bulldogs was the football club that gave me an opportunity to realise a dream and become a professional sportsman in the NRL. We won a premiership together, and no-one can ever take the joy of that away. The man I am today is not the man I was back then, but because of that journey I confronted my issues, worked on my mental health and found the strength and boundaries I needed within Islam. I am proud of who I am now. And back in 2013, I was ready to play NRL.

* * *

That year was a rollercoaster of emotions. Behind any chance of success was a lot of struggling and hard work, both physical and mental. It had been five years since I'd stepped out on a footy field to play the game I grew up loving – rugby league. I had just hit my straps in the international game with the All Blacks and I had been playing with ease in union so it might have been easier to stay in New Zealand. But I had to step up and deal with any unfinished emotional business. And I wanted to keep my word, which I had given to Nick Politis and David Gyngell, who I had talked to years earlier and promised that one day I would pull on a Roosters jersey. That time was now.

I could definitely feel the pressure and excitement leading up to that first game. I was determined to prove to my teammates that all the fuss about my return was warranted and that I could still play in the NRL and add value to their team. I never thought it would be a walk in the park, but I also hadn't counted on coming up against two of the best straight off the bat. I don't know why I hadn't; I knew the calibre of players in the NRL. And then it was on. Big Sam Burgess came at me off a goalline dropout and ran straight over the top of me before Greg Inglis ran riot. It was the dose of reality I needed. That game not only fired me up and gave me more of a motivation to show my worth, it made me realise a couple of other things. I needed to be stronger in the gym and I needed to be really mentally tough to offset the young warriors who wanted to mark their territory and come after me. I was a target and I had to be greater than them.

With these thoughts in my mind, I started meeting our strength and conditioning coach Keegan Smith first thing in the morning for extra weight and strength sessions before our scheduled training. And I started using visualisations to sharpen my mind. Each week I would visualise what could happen on the field against various opponents. I'd done this a little bit with the All Blacks so it wasn't entirely new to me, and it worked. Before that first game, I had never really understood how individual rivalries could elevate your efforts but when Sammy Burgess and Greg Inglis smashed me in the face, it hit me! I will always be thankful to them, the fans and the media too. They loved what they saw that night in that game and never let me forget it. All that helped me play harder and eventually took my game to another level.

The Roosters had finished near the bottom of the ladder in 2012 and that proved the catalyst for the hunger in the squad I stepped into. The team connection and culture at the Roosters was impressive and I was living clean and going above and beyond in training. I saw that second effort in my teammates; it was embedded in everyone and so it was the norm. There were a lot of similarities between this Rooster side and the Chiefs team of 2012 and that felt good. There were a lot of hungry young guys like Jared Waerea-Hargreaves, Roger Tuivasa-Sheck, Sam Moa, Mitchell Aubusson, Mitchell Pearce, Frank-Paul Nu'uausala and a young future NSW and Australian captain Boyd Cordner, alongside Anthony Minichiello, James Maloney, Michael Jennings, Daniel Tupou, Shaun Kenny-Dowall and Jake Friend to name just a few.

But even with all that talent, we still needed to believe in ourselves as a team. With the coaches' demands for the perfect game defensively and our natural flair on attack, we started getting a feel for our style of play and found that self-belief in ourselves and in each other. Being really successful means doing those one per cent things you don't see on TV. Every week we reviewed everything, and earning your teammates' respect in those sessions translated to putting in the effort in the game.

As the season went on, we could feel something special brewing, but through all that we felt the same happening at Souths – both our sides were having seasons to remember. I couldn't shake the thought that Russell Crowe's team was waiting to pounce and I believed we'd be the teams in the grand final together. I didn't watch many other games that year but I made sure I watched every Rabbitohs game to keep tabs on what they were up to. If we were going to do the impossible and win the trophy, I knew we had to beat this team to do it. But I had a deep sense of belief in the Roosters players and our team energy, and that belief never wavered no matter the scoreline.

Rusty Crowe is like Nick Politis, he is the lynchpin of the club behind the scenes and, just like with Nick, I had real respect for him. He seems the kind of guy you want to play for and every week Greg Inglis and Sammy

Burgess would come out and play their hearts out for the team, the fans and for Russell.

The Roosters and Souths headed into round twenty-six, the last round of that year before finals footy, in first and second place on the table. Whoever won this game would not only go into the finals as a slight favourite but they'd go in with the confidence of knowing that they had just beaten their main rival and be crowned the minor premiers.

This was one of my favourite games of the year. It had everything – pressure, aggression, skill, brute force and two teams determined to win. And it all unfolded in front of a crowd of more than 60,000 fans at ANZ Stadium.

Souths and the Roosters are rugby league foundation clubs and that night the two teams put on a show that I was blessed to be a part of. Trent Robinson put me in the centres to defend as Shaun Kenny-Dowall was out injured. It was a massive task, because the majority of their tries had been scored down their left edge, with Greg Inglis their chief attacker. I had spent years playing centre in rugby so I was up for the job. It's simple, right? Stop GI, stop them.

Well, stopping Greg Inglis is not so easy! Their first assault was on our twenty-metre line. I saw Greg Inglis screaming around the back, nothing I didn't know was coming considering the amount of footage I'd studied of him and Souths. One of the big Burgess boys sets the play because of his size and it is usually a fast one, and then the ball goes through Adam Reynolds' hands out back to Inglis, who then has plenty of space to work his magic.

I have spoken about the mental warfare that happens on the field – well, this time it was my turn to make a statement. The ball left Reynolds' hands and I timed it beautifully and set out to make a massive shot on Inglis, their best player, to set the tone from then on. Well, I definitely made a statement . . . that Greg Inglis is bloody hard to tackle! He bumped me off and ran through another would-be defender on his way to score the game's first points. It wasn't the best way to start the game. I was under the post and Minichiello was talking to me, but I was in my own world. I remember thinking, *Far out, that is definitely making the highlights reel but not in my favour*, but then I told myself there was still seventy minutes left to play. I had to make some of my own plays to offset Inglis. I can't remember GI coming down outside too many times for the rest of the game because every time I could see a play unfolding where he'd look like getting the ball, I was there ahead of our defence line, screaming at him to let him know he might bump me off again but he better be ready for it because I was coming. Alhamdulillah, he didn't, because I don't think I could have lived with the embarrassment of getting bumped off twice in one game.

At the end of that game, the highlights reel was full of remarkable moments from both teams and I was pleased that I had made some positive impacts. But winning that game was only the beginning, our eyes were on the real prize – holding up the Provan-Summons Trophy at the end of the grand final.

The next game was a hard-fought game of attrition against Manly and we won that 4–0. Young gun Roger Tuivasa-Sheck scored the game's only try. I always knew he was destined for greatness as he has freakish skills topped off with a humble head on his young shoulders. I look forward to seeing him take his talents over to the fifteen-man game of rugby because the world deserves to see talent like his.

We had the week off and then we were going up against my old Bulldogs teammate Willie Mason's Newcastle Knights. But during that week, I went out to dinner and ate some seafood that didn't sit right at the time and then got worse. I ended up not being able to hold anything down. Food poisoning was not the prep I needed, and I couldn't train because I was so sick. I wasn't sure I would be able to suit up, but I made it to the game and although I had the utmost faith in our side I knew I couldn't miss it for the boys. I struggled through warm-up and by kick-off I was hoping I'd have enough energy to make it through.

Early in the game, a young player from Newcastle tried to put it on me to fight. I don't know if it was a tactic, because it didn't really happen to me very often. I always tried to play hard and fair but his provocation failed to do what he might have hoped. I wasn't intimidated; I fired up and suddenly had the energy and motivation to play with more determination. We won that game and I was lucky enough to get the Man of the Match award. We were off to the big dance!

To my and many others' surprise, twenty-four hours later, in the other major semi-final, Souths got beaten by Manly in a massive upset. This meant we were playing a grand final against the Sea Eagles and we'd already beaten them three times that year, so we went in deserving favourites.

Deep down I was confident we could get it done. And the truth was, because it was Manly, I wasn't as nervous as I would have been if we were going head to head with South Sydney. I made a silly error early, which led to them scoring the opening try. But that's the luxury of playing a team sport and something you don't get in the ring. If I am in a fight and I do something silly, I can be dropped in the opening round. But on the footy field, with your teammates around you, you can redeem yourself and collectively work your way back into the contest. We had a great side led by Sam Moa and Jared Waerea-Hargreaves in the forwards and though Manly dominated physically in the first half, thanks to some James Maloney and Daniel Tupou brilliance, we went into the half-time break 8–6 up. I had slowly worked my way back into the game and could feel my involvement increasing. During the break, the coach and a few players were talking but I was in my own head again.

I remember it as if it was yesterday; there was so much emotion in the sheds and I was sitting there talking to myself, saying, *Still forty minutes to go, follow a bad deed with a good deed, back yourself, be in the play and always say Alhamdulillah.*

We hit out in the second half but everything seemed to go Manly's way and they shot out to a ten-point lead. Usually it's impossible to come back from a scoreline like that in such a big game, but this Roosters team wasn't made up of the usual players following the usual script. That game with that awesome group of men will always hold a special place in my sporting memories because of the courage we showed in sticking to our style of play. The way the team held tight and pushed the boundaries despite what looked like insurmountable adversity was incredible. Not only did we come back to win the game 26–18, we did it with the style that only players who dared to dream could. When the final whistle blew, I dropped to the ground into sujūd to thank my Creator for making yet another dream come true.

The year of 2013 was by far the most daunting year in my sporting career, even more so than when I'd been a rookie stepping into first-grade NRL. After five years out of the game, I was about to face up to the club, teammates and fans I had walked out on. The pressure of expectations, my own and others', along with the very vocal wish of some for me to fail, meant there was a lot to deal with. But my deep sense of drive and dedication, along with the support of my teammates and people like Nick Politis and David Gyngell saw me enjoy one of my most successful years, both on and off the field. As a sportsman, I was part of an NRL premiership-winning team and I was named the Roosters Players' Player, something very special to me. I was also named the International Player of the Year. That year also saw me meet the future mother of my children and I would come through the season with no major injuries. Alhamdulillah.

CHAPTER 11

The coaches

Over the years, I have played under a fair few coaches and sussed out what works well for me. People always ask who was the best, and the truth is I learned something from them all – even if it was what didn't work. I've mentioned some of them earlier, but here are my thoughts on some of the coaches who made an impact (in no particular order).

Steve Hansen (All Blacks coach, 2012–2019)

Steve is a very good people person. I don't think he taught me anything new from a skill perspective; his strength is his ability to motivate players, to compel them to be at their best, and he did that with me.

I learned from him that, along with the skills and the mindset, getting the player to be at their greatest is hugely important. The All Blacks environment is a blessed one, with the best players in the world and an amazing array of talents. One guy can jump in a lineout twice his height; one can sidestep twenty men; another is a kicker; and yet another is someone who nails everyone in a tackle.

The depth in the All Blacks team is unbelievable, and I think most rugby heads would agree that New Zealand, boiled down to the wider squad of thirty-two All Blacks and then again to the twenty-three Test-playing squad, has the most depth of talent of any rugby-playing nation. That's why if you get injured in the All Blacks there's someone ready to take your place, and they will be determined to keep that spot and not want to hand it back. He might be your best mate. Doesn't matter. This is business. The business of elite-level sport.

So, besides a solid game plan and being able to push the limits of each player, a good coach knows that every player has a unique personality and each will respond to a coach's talk in a different way. Steve knew that and he was an unbelievable motivator, always the one guy in the room who could get the best out of me.

I really admire Steve because of his persistence in the face of failure. He didn't let defeat stop him and with this persistence he went from his struggles with Wales and then came back to the All Blacks. After losing that 2007 quarter-final to France, he didn't give up on his dream of becoming senior coach. The All Blacks would end up winning two World Cups with him as coach and he would go on to become the greatest international rugby coach of all time. The statistics of his reign back that up. I will always respect that resilience and the journey he went on. The only thing that bothered me after a while was that Steve didn't always hold himself to the same accountability and honesty that he placed on me and others.

The only thing I would have loved Steve to have done during his tenure as All Blacks coach would have been to bring in an assistant coach of Māori or Pacific Island heritage to mentor and teach his coaching knowledge and skill set to. Instead, that opportunity was lost. That is my only criticism of his reign.

One more word on Steve 'Shag' Hansen: he's married to a Māori. I don't know how he got her, because she's beautiful. But he could talk underwater, Shag, and I think that was the winning way of him. He spoke from the heart.

Dave Rennie (Chiefs coach, 2012–2017)

The Chiefs won back-to-back Super titles in 2012 and 2013. Dave Rennie is a very strong-minded individual, and that 2012 season was awesome. Dave is huge on culture; he had to blend and bond a group of guys mostly from outside of the Hamilton–Waikato region and he did that well.

His focus was that simple game: forwards lay the foundation, backs get involved whenever we see fit. The thing I loved about Rens is that he backed me as a leader and he stressed what I could do for the boys, especially the younger players. I knew what to do, but I needed someone to empower me to do it. I didn't do all that tough stuff with the youngies; they need encouragement and they need to be instilled with confidence. That's what inspires them to go out and play well.

Rens expected my leadership role to continue off the field too. He involved me in everything, and naturally I felt an extra obligation to live up to his expectations. Maybe he deliberately planned this? Whatever. It worked.

I remember our semi-final against the Crusaders in 2012 was like a final. That game. Man, I bet it is etched in every Chiefs player's memory.

My combo with Aaron Cruden was perfect. We could read each other's minds. Brodie Retallick was just a youngster then. But he showed why he was destined to be an All Blacks lock great. That young man had everything, including no shortage of the necessary mongrel his position requires. Tim Nanai-Williams (my cousin) was on the wing (and just like his older brother, was very unlucky not to play for the All Blacks – I would love to have seen him on the world stage in that black jersey). Sam Cane, future All Blacks captain and a real nice guy, was there.

And Liam 'Hunga' Messam was there – he had been in and out of the All Blacks, and I don't think deserved that treatment. He never gave less than 100 per cent every game he played. Maybe some of the coaches didn't like his flair, his unpredictability, but it wins more matches than it loses. Rens rated him, though, and New Zealand rugby sevens coach Gordon Tietjens includes Liam Messam in his greatest rugby sevens team of all time. Hunga and I were inseparable off the field. Brothers. I think having a coach of colour really helped bond us. We are still very close, like all those Chiefs boys are to this day.

Trent Robinson (Roosters coach, 2013–present day)

Trent Robinson was only thirty-six and in his first year coaching NRL when I met him. Robbo was on his way back from England to take up the Roosters gig, and he came via Japan to see me as I was contracted to return to league. Robbo's strength was his humility and his approachable personality. His door was always open, and I felt I could have a yarn with him anytime.

We really connected at that meeting in Japan. I appreciated his holistic approach to footy. In one sense he was old school, yet he was new school in some of his thinking. I loved that he came and watched me play rugby in Japan, where I was doing little grubber kicks, throwing outrageous offloads. I knew going back to league was going to mean a different structure, but he always wanted me to play my own game, which means playing with my eyes up and looking for opportunities, or creating them.

I also got on well with our attack coach, Jason Taylor, who would say to me, 'What were you doing there?' and 'Why did you do that?'. I'd tell him, 'I saw this, so I did that,' sort of thing. He said, 'You've got to get back to position because we need to run this line.' So, we had a few awkward conversations, but I consider them conversations of growth.

I brought my rugby mindset to league as a back rower: always scoping, always watching where the play was heading, looking for where the gaps were. If I had to go from one side of the field to the other, then I would. It didn't matter to me if it wasn't in the league playbook. The objective was and always is to win.

What I loved about Robbo was that as long as I was doing those little one-percenters on defence, getting back in position, breaking out then getting back, he supported me. If I was doing all those little hard-yard things – the things the people at home don't see on the television screen – then he left it up to me what I did on attack. Robbo never said, 'This is the way it's done and always been done and it's going to stay that way.' I have so much respect for him for that.

Wayne Bennett

I have a lot of respect for Wayne Bennett. He is one of the best motivators I've ever had. He only coached me once, with the Kiwis against his own Australian Kangaroos. As soon as he got to our camp he said, 'Come with me, Sonny. We're going for a coffee.' I'm thinking, *Wow. This is none other than* the *Wayne Bennett*. I was peaking at the time, on fire with the Doggies, and had been injured a bit in the previous two tests against the Aussies.

He said, 'You think you've done your Kiwi jersey proud? Well, have another think about it.' He was saying that I had to step it up again. He would come down the back of the bus and sit and yarn with the players. We loved him. I ended up playing one of my best games in the black jersey after that chat.

Because we represent so much out there in the field, coaches who understand the connection between Māori, Aboriginal and Polynesian boys are usually the most successful ones. Wayne respected and understood them.

Apparently he reached out to me when I left the Doggies. Unfortunately the message never reached me. If there was one man who could have changed my mind, or who might have understood what I was doing, it was Wayne Bennett.

Steve Folkes (Canterbury-Bankstown coach, 1998–2008)

There's my Bulldogs coach, Steve Folkes – he passed away in 2018, sadly. He believed in me from the start, this eighteen-year-old kid from New Zealand. He was the first coach to let me play a roving position. Even if I wore the number 11 jersey – which is the right-back edge, and you're supposed to stay there – he'd expect me to get the ball on both sides. He figured the more often I got the ball in my hands, the better the chance to break the line with my unconventional play. He just let me go out and play my game.

Shortly after the news broke that I'd been caught drink-driving, we had to go to a charity event, or maybe it was a club promotion. Steve came to tell me that the media were waiting outside the club and I should come in his car. When we arrived at the event, the cameras were clicking, the microphones were at the ready, but Steve just walked me past them all into the club. Not much was said, but his support at that time meant a lot to me.

My relationship with Folkesy ended with my abrupt departure from the Bulldogs. I wasn't at war with him or the club. Things happened that I didn't like, but I didn't have the maturity to talk it out or speak up.

I was such a fan of Steve's and now he's gone I can't ever sit down and talk with him man to man about it all. I am sad about that.

Todd Blackadder (Crusaders coach, 2008–2016)

I loved Todd Blackadder's coaching at the Crusaders. He was another coach who just let me play. That 2011 season was a tough one, especially in light of the dramatic effect the February earthquake had on both the citizens of Christchurch and us players. I know I was unsettled by the quakes and the horror we saw. The team fell at the last hurdle, against the Queensland Reds.

Playing for the Reds was my close buddy, a brother, Quade Cooper. Funnily enough, our friendship started about this time. He is like a younger brother (though he looks older than me!). Although I couldn't see it then, as I am so competitive, I look back at that night with happiness because although we lost, my brother won, so essentially I won too.

Even though I made lifetime friends with people like Ben and Owen Franks, Sam Whitelock, Kieran Read and Izzy Dagg, to name a few, while at the Crusaders, I wasn't enjoying the long periods away from my mum and the family. Todd understood this and yet he always had confidence in my ability, which I appreciated. He didn't try to bog me down; he just told me to play my natural game, be aggressive and, yes, offload, but be smart about it.

When I arrived, he helped me believe in myself. The hardest thing about leaving the Crusaders was telling

Todd, because we had such a good relationship. I give thanks to my Creator for blessing me with such a good coach and a good man.

Seeing his son, Ethan, reach the heights he has in New Zealand rugby and make the All Blacks team is no surprise to me. Growing up in that household and carrying the genes of his old man made it inevitable.

Tana Umaga (Toulon coach, 2008–2009)

Tana is a man I had a lot of respect for even before I met him. His support and belief in my ability to play rugby brought out the best in me, on and off the field. He is a former All Blacks captain and I got to know him well when he threw me a lifeline after I started to self-destruct at the Bulldogs. Without his faith in me, I am not sure where I would be now. I was heading for burnout and on a bad path when he reached out and made me believe I could make the switch from league to union.

Tana's strength is his loyalty to the boys. He always puts the team members first, and with his experience being the first Islander captain for the All Blacks, he understands the pressures young Islanders face and the struggles we have with everything that comes with it. I consider Tana a friend for life and I'm grateful for my time learning from him.

Philippe Saint-André (Toulon coach, 2009–2011)

At a time when I was so caught up in trying to learn every little detail and every new rule in a game I'd never played, Philippe taught me, or reminded me, of something special: to simply step back, take a breath and remember your strengths. He never wanted me to overthink the game and always pushed me to play with my instincts and back myself.

I guess when you have the likes of Jonny Wilkinson inside and Tana outside, you don't need to think, just listen, watch and you'll be okay. As I was. Philippe has had a lot of success and if it wasn't for my desire to play for the All Blacks, maybe things could have been a lot different. Who knows what might have happened? The country of France could have ended up being called home.

Brian McDermott (Toronto Wolfpack coach, 2019–2020)

It's not every day you get to work with a coach who has headed up five Super League premiership-winning teams. Brian is the most successful Super League coach in history and it was apparent to me straight away why he was so successful – because he is always thinking of ways to improve our side by understanding our strengths and the opposition's weaknesses. He is a realist who understood we lacked a bit of depth in our team, but that didn't stop him from coming up with ways for us to not only compete but win games. Although we didn't have the luxury of a big squad or younger players to pick from, I went into each game with the sense that we could compete. Brian is a very good man who always had all players in the locker room fully committed. I am disappointed that I only got to play for him on a few occasions. I think if the circumstances had been different, with a bit of time and a few more resources, Brian could have led that Toronto team somewhere special. He was looking after the team in a really tough period and the disruption of Covid was a challenge but he was always supportive and honest with all of us foreigners. I look forward to seeing him as a head coach of another club, maybe even in the NRL, soon.

Gordon Tietjens (New Zealand All Blacks rugby sevens coach)

Going to the Olympic Games was a dream I never thought would be possible. But then one day, I set my sights on making it happen. To succeed, I needed to know all that was required to make the cut and understand the demands of the game. Who better to ask than the most respected coach in rugby sevens history? Gordon 'Titch' Tietjens has led the New Zealand team to the most tournament wins in the history of the game. When I spoke to Gordon, he was very clear on what I had to do and although I knew it would be a massive challenge, with his guidance and support, I knew I had the best chance possible of making the Olympic rugby sevens team. Without his belief and backing, I don't think I would have made it to the standard needed. Achieving that goal is something I am very proud of. Yes, injury meant my Olympic dream ended badly, but I will always be able to say I was coached by the best coach in that field. For twenty-two years, he guided the New Zealand rugby sevens and in that time they won twelve World Series titles, four Commonwealth Games gold medals and two World Cups.

Craig Bellamy (Melbourne Storm coach, 2003–present day)

The only coach I've never been coached by who I strongly admire is Craig Bellamy. After fifteen years at the Melbourne Storm, his record of winning premierships is impressive. But the aspect I admire most about Craig is his ability to give fringe players and players other clubs have given up on a second chance. Not only does he bring out the best in these players, he helps guide them on the path to become world class. A coach who can do that is one who understands that every player is different and coaches them accordingly to unite a team.

* * *

I think the key takeaway about coaching for me – and I have said it earlier – is that the best coach is one who understands that a team is made up of a range of personalities, and what works for one person won't necessarily work for another. You have to be a true people person and understand how to get the best out of each individual player. But you can't just use the same formula and the same tactic every time. Doesn't matter if it is an under-16s team or the All Blacks, you need to know your players so you can maximise their strengths and help them to overcome any weaknesses. You need to listen, observe and understand each player so you can work out how to unite them to play as a fierce, competitive team. And that is a winning combination.

CHAPTER 12

Going for gold

You know by now that sport has been my focus since I was a kid. At first, athletics and rugby were equally as important. Me, Johnny and my sisters Niall and Denise were all members of Roskill South Athletics Club. I was a sprinter and high jumper. I think I still hold the club high-jump record for ten-year-olds at 1.43 metres. But when I was about twelve it became all about playing rugby league in the NRL, followed by the challenge of rugby union and making the All Blacks team. Then, in 2015, a new challenge worked its way into my brain: the Olympics!

You could say I am a very driven individual. I have found one of the keys to my happiness and self-development is to set goals for myself. Whether it is aiming for the Olympics or being with my kids, I always take the same approach – full steam ahead and leave no stone unturned in order to achieve that goal.

As youngsters, most of us get excited about the Olympics; I know I did. It is the mega sports event that stops most of the world. So when it was announced that rugby sevens would be included in Rio 2016, I thought first of the challenge and then the buzz of being there as an athlete. And it was special to know my sister was on the same journey.

People see Sonny for the amazing athlete he is – the two Rugby World Cups, playing for the Kiwis, winning NRL titles for two different clubs, a New Zealand Super Rugby title with the Chiefs, being crowned the New Zealand heavyweight boxing champion. As a sports fanatic myself, I couldn't have asked for a better role model than my own brother. I guess I kind of lived my journey alongside his in getting to represent New Zealand in two different sports. But I'm not saying I'm the female Sonny Bill!

He is the best of the best when it comes to New Zealand athletes, and I admire everything he's done on the field. But it's off the field that I admire him most: the good person he is, the kind, caring, giving, humorous personality that only those close to him know.

Speaking about him I get quite emotional, because he holds such a special place in my heart. I remember when I was nineteen and did my ACL joint. I always made the national touch

squad, and coming back from that injury was the first time
I missed out. I was absolutely heartbroken, having lost the only
thing I was madly passionate about. I wasn't great at school.
Sport was my passion. What was I supposed to do now?

Sonny, who was playing for the Crusaders, told me and my
partner, Tama, to come down to Christchurch and stay with
him. He said, 'You can work for me part-time,' and he got me a
personal trainer. So I looked after the household and I trained.
My trainer got me into the best shape I'd ever been. When I went
back to touch rugby I was the fastest, fittest, strongest in the
team and got my spot back.

Now, no-one knows about this, but Sonny paid for me and my
partner to go on this trip around Europe with the New Zealand
Academy team and we went to Spain, Italy, England, Wales and
taught their national touch teams, and we played in the European
championship. We were with such a great bunch of people, and
I learned to love the game again. That trip cost $8000 each. My
bro gave us $16,000 and he didn't tell a soul. He just wanted me
to get my love for the game back.

When my brother saw me down, he helped me up. That
speaks volumes to me over and above what he has done on the
field. – Niall Williams

I wasn't sure getting into the national rugby sevens team
would even be possible. I really had to sit down and think
about what I was going to do next.

To me, he was Sonny my husband and closest friend first and
foremost. I didn't take any notice of him being famous. He put
enough pressure on himself in trying to stay injury-free, doing
constant rehab exercises and treatments. You could never
question his determination and willpower. So when Sonny set his
sights on the Olympics, I knew he would do it. – Alana Williams

Being an Olympian really means being the best of the
best, and for someone like me, who loved pushing myself,
mastering a new game and learning something new, it
was the ultimate challenge. The very best sportspeople
ever have also been Olympians – people I admire like
Usain Bolt, Muhammad Ali, Naim Süleymanoğlu,
Hakeem Olajuwon, Hicham El Guerrouj, Saïd Aouita,
Michael Jordan, 'Sugar' Ray Leonard and Mohamed
Farah. The chance to win an Olympic medal wasn't
something I thought would ever happen for me, but with
the rugby sevens making its debut in the 2016 Rio de
Janeiro Olympics, that dream seemed . . . possible.

So that was it. I locked on to that goal and spent most
of that year doing everything I could to make the squad.
I reached out to a few people, including New Zealand
head coach Gordon Tietjens, to find out more about
fitness levels and expectations, and I talked to some mates
I'd played with at the Chiefs, like Liam Messam. I didn't
know how I'd go and so was nervous about it at first, but

once I had committed I was sure as hell going to go my hardest. I wanted to make the team but I wanted to do it well. There was no way I wanted to let anyone down. Like with the All Blacks, you have to honour the players who have been before you and pave the way for those to come. I knew I had the skill set, but rugby sevens is fast moving and fast running and there is nowhere to hide, so it requires full-on conditioning.

I have always trained hard and gone above and beyond what was expected of me, but Gordon Tietjens's fitness regime was the toughest I've ever done since my introduction to professional sport in my Bulldogs days. The conditioning levels were insane – but, then, the Olympics are a whole other level. To get there I had to play in six World Rugby Sevens Series tournaments to show my worth to the team. It is not until you play rugby sevens that you understand the demands asked of you out there. It is pretty much a sprint for seven minutes a half. Day-to-day training is gruelling and you have to commit. I truly gave it my all because I wanted to hear my name called out in that Olympic team.

There was a three-day camp in January 2016, and I lost three kilos in the prep for it. The first day we did an hour of fitness games after a beep test (used to measure aerobic power) and I knew I still had work to do. I wasn't where I wanted to be at that point, but that just made me train harder.

I've always had a sort of fear of playing against small, nippy guys because they're more elusive and fast, and usually pretty strong too. This was what I saw around me: a whole bunch of small guys – compared to me, at least. And the fitness required was a different kind of fitness; people don't understand the huge difference between fifteen-man and seven-man rugby. Sevens is so aerobic. That's why a game is two halves of seven minutes each, with a two-minute half-time break. You're running, tackling and being tackled the whole time. Missing one key tackle can cost your team the match.

I was trying to find the balance between being my usual physical self and playing a whole new game in which I had only six teammates to rely on and all that space to play in and be played against. To my delight, my offload worked in rugby sevens, and so did my physical tackles.

Titch was an amazing coach, a fanatic on fitness and very encouraging of me. His sessions were gruelling, but I just got on with things, and though I was worried, I was more than ready to make my debut in Wellington at the end of January. We won that tournament (yes, an offload or two and a couple of tries featured). It wasn't easy going, that's for sure, and I played in some serious rugby sevens tournaments, but was also sidelined by a few injuries. I played in the Sydney tournament, and we won the final against Australia.

And then, in July 2016, I was named in the All Blacks Sevens Olympic team. Alhamdulillah! Another goal achieved. But I wasn't the only member of the Williams family heading to Rio that year. I was really proud to make the team, but I was even prouder of my little sister Niall. She is a mother of two and when she first set her eyes on Rio, she wasn't contracted to any club. She would get up really early to train, spend the day looking after her daughters, and then train late at night. I think resilience and dedication must be in our genes, because we both did whatever it took to make the New Zealand Olympic team. Mum and Dad were proudest of all.

I was loving everything about playing sevens. I just wanted to stay healthy and injury-free and work with my teammates to bring the gold medal home. But I wasn't under any illusions: this competition was going to be fierce.

* * *

Walking into the Olympic Village in Rio was amazing. It's a massive place; you wouldn't believe the size of it. All these big high-rise accommodation 'hotels' had been built to house over 10,000 athletes. Walking around the village was a surreal experience for me, seeing all these athletes from different countries of every complexion and size – and, of course, with that heightened air of being physically aware of the space they're occupying that's common to all athletes.

We had designated hotels for each country in sections of the village, and New Zealand was sharing theirs with Ireland. The logistics of looking after and moving people around was mind-blowing. Some things worked well, but other things were tested just by the huge number of people. I remember there was a limited number of bikes to ride to the food hall. We soon learned you either had to grab a bike early or walk to the food hall and then eat fast so you could score a bike afterwards. That's what teammate Akira Ioane and I used to do.

Man, athletes give off their own aura, and I loved just riding around checking it all out. We'd pass a guy doing karate on the grass, someone doing stretches, a guy shadow-boxing, and that was where I saw an Olympic walker for the first time ever. I must have missed the walkers when watching the Games over the years on TV, and seeing that run/walk for the first time made us laugh because it looked so awkward. I wasn't laughing in a disrespectful way; it just looked funny with that hip action. It's so technical and the speed is impressive, but I know I couldn't do it; I would break into a run.

We heard rumours that the American basketball team had their own big luxury boat offshore to live on, and it turned out to be true. While most of the American athletes were in the dorms like us, the men's and women's basketballers were on a massive cruise ship. They'd come into the village every once in a while, superstars at the peak of their fitness and fame. One day, Akira and I were riding around and he went around a corner before me. I followed and nearly crashed into him. He'd stopped dead. Staring.

There, walking towards us, with no massive crowds of fans or minders, was Team USA, the American men's basketball team. Unfortunately, we didn't have our phones so we couldn't take any pictures. We caught ourselves staring at these exceptional athletes as we were avid fans. Kevin Durant got close to us and he stopped and said, 'How are you, guys? Y'all cool?' He greeted us and acknowledged us and it was a nice moment because I really liked that guy.

I loved my time in that village. Spain's hotel was next to ours. We saw Rafael Nadal and got a photo with him. Nice guy. I didn't know much about tennis, but I did recognise his achievements. Another time, I saw retired sprinter John Steffensen, who'd won a silver medal for Australia, in the food hall. He was at the Olympics in a mentoring role. John had a name for being fired up and calling out racism. Being a black man, he'd been on the receiving end too many times, so to see him now on the board of Athletics Australia was a sign that things were changing for the better. We knew each other, so had a good catch-up. He was staying with Usain Bolt and he invited me to come hang out with them later that night. I wanted to include some of my rugby boys, but I didn't want to impose on the big man, who was competing soon.

Usain Bolt is huge on the world stage and that was respected by the Olympics. He had an entire hotel floor to himself. Our whole team shared a floor. I turned up and we had a mad yarn. We talked about sport and politics. What I really like about him is the way he acknowledges everyone who is part of putting an event together. On the track he always gives a nod to the young kids who clean up the starting blocks after he runs or the volunteers who make things run smoothly. On the big stage, where it would be so easy to make it all about him, he takes time to make a young kid's day with a fist bump and a smile. That is what I really admire about him. It was a pretty enlightening chat. He is an impressive dude. Smart, likeable and funny, he was very aware of his position in the world, but also respectful to everyone, no matter who they were. 'It's one thing my parents would be really upset and hate about me, if I changed and stopped having respect. My parents would be crazy,' Usain said in an interview once. I know about that!

It was awesome to spend time with Usain, and as well as the chat, I do remember his feet. They were like huge plates. I figured he must have walked barefoot his whole life and he got his speed pushing off those big feet. The man is a champion and would go on to win three gold medals at that Olympics – in the 100 metres, the 200 metres and the 4 × 100-metres relay. And he'd done that at the previous two Olympics. He is definitely one of the greatest athletes of all time, and he worked hard, trained hard and pushed himself to become that. That's inspiring.

As well as the thrill of seeing sporting superstars everywhere you look, a big part of the excitement of the Olympics is the Opening Ceremony. Every athlete competing at the Games wants to be part of it, and I did too. But you can never lose sight of why you are there – to compete and to win. So I decided to stay at the hotel and watch the ceremony on television because I wanted to rest my legs. Now that I'd achieved the goal of being an Olympian, I had moved on to the next goal: winning gold.

* * *

On the first day of competition, the nerves kicked in. This was what I had focused on for a year. We were playing Japan at Deodoro Stadium and in the second half, I went into a tackle and didn't get up. I'd ruptured my Achilles tendon and had to be helped from the field. I was devastated, and more than anything I felt bad that I had let the team down. We lost that game 14–12 and would end up finishing fifth in the Olympic competition overall. There was no medal of any colour coming home with me. I was pretty gutted about that for the team and because of all the sacrifices that had been made to get to those Games. But that is sport. And elite sport takes no prisoners.

My sister Niall was there to help me through it. And the drama didn't end with the Achilles injury. The next thing I knew, I was hit with a stomach bug and diarrhoea. There was a little storage room at the back of the hotel where I had to kind of quarantine myself from the boys so they didn't get infected.

But the good news is there was an Olympic medal in the family. Niall and the women's rugby sevens team won the silver medal. Me and my family were so proud of her! She posted a message on social media encouraging me after her final:

This journey has been full of ups and downs, ins and outs, the known and unknown . . . but I wouldn't have wanted to do it with anyone else but him by my side. We both started this journey as a brother and sister who wanted to prove themselves in the [sevens] rugby game and are now able to call ourselves Olympians after representing New Zealand rugby sevens on the biggest sporting stage ever! No-one can ever take this moment we shared away from us and it's something we will treasure forever. Although his ended the way it did, I know he's not feeling sorry for himself and will be back better and stronger; with family, faith and will on his side, he is on the right track back. Silver wasn't the colour we wanted but a podium finish is nothing short of *amazing*. This medal is as much his as it is mine for the fact I wouldn't be here if it wasn't for the love, faith and support he's shown me from day one. Love you, bro. – Niall Williams

Love you too, sis. People can forget that disappointments don't just affect the athlete. Your family take that ride with you and are just as invested in achieving your goal. I was so proud of Niall but I was hurting for myself. I have to admit that after all the effort, the training and the preparation this Olympic injury hit hard. I'd wanted a medal so badly for myself and the team and once my Achilles went, I still hoped the team could play on without me and achieve gold. It wasn't to be.

Sonny trained and trained to make that New Zealand rugby sevens team so he could compete in Rio. He always put the training in, no matter what, but he also studied notes on the game's finer points and he was constantly away: gone for two or three weeks, home for two weeks, off again.

At the time I was thinking, *Why did this happen to Sonny, a dream destroyed after so much hard work?* We turned to our faith, looking for a reason. When he had the tests he was told by the doctors he had an injury that would take nine months to heal. So, he was at home in New Zealand doing rehab and, typical Sonny, was back to fitness in seven months. – Alana Williams

It took months to recover physically, but mentally it took almost as long. I couldn't train so I had to work hard to keep from sliding into a depression like I had previously. So much of what I do is about my physicality and training that I still struggle when I can't. Islam helped me deal with that. My daily prayers, keeping focused on the moment and being grateful for all that I had done and all that I had. My body was taking longer to recover and injuries were taking a toll. I knew the day was coming when I had some big decisions to make, but I wasn't quite there yet.

CHAPTER 13

Not ready to stop . . . yet

As I got older, my work ethic continued to improve. I knew what I had to do to play or box at my best. My motivation and desire to stay at the top meant I pushed myself. I was always looking at ways to make that one per cent difference, both on and off the field. That is what I had to do, both as far as my physical body was concerned but also for my mental wellbeing. On the field, that second effort can make a difference in a game; off-field, it meant the dreaded ice baths, stretches and yoga, on top of the usual training.

I am a team man, so if I can't train or perform as well as I usually do because of injury, it bothers me.

Dealing with injury and pain has been a big part of my career and any pro sportsperson will tell you the same: it goes with the territory. I always wanted to give myself the best chance so it meant countless operations and rehab and always pushing myself to recover quickly. In 2010, just before I went to New Zealand and started playing with the Crusaders, I had a routine clean-up of my knee to make sure I was fit and ready to go. After the op, the doctor told me he thought I could get it to the point where I would be able to play the 2011 World Cup but he couldn't guarantee anything after that. I decided I would do all I could to prove him wrong.

Many operations later, fast-forward to the start of the 2019 World Cup year. I had the regular routine check-ups to make sure I was in the best shape I could be. After some scans came back, I was told that with the way my knee was looking, I should probably start thinking about life post footy. The realities of that conversation hit me hard and got my mind racing. In the previous four years, I had dealt with an Achilles tear, a ruptured AC joint, broken bones in my shoulder, a few concussions and the old not-so-faithful knee on top of other small niggles, and every time I had done what needed to be done to be able to step back up. The mention of a possible end to my playing career was confronting. I still had the dream to play a part in winning three consecutive Rugby World Cups with the All Blacks, alongside Kieran Read, Owen Franks and Sam Whitelock, and this conversation seemed to be putting a line through that. I sat with those thoughts and then I realised I didn't have to agree to this outcome. I was going to put my faith in my Creator and in focusing on the one per cent wins and do everything possible to achieve this World Cup goal at the end of the year. If I spent two hours on the field, I'd follow that up with at least three hours preparing for the next day just to be able to train. I'd stand in the ocean for twenty minutes, no matter what the weather conditions or the temperature – cold, raining, three degrees, windy, it didn't matter. I'd get on a trigger-point roller and work my muscles before doing thirty to sixty minutes of yoga at home. To top it all off, I'd use the ice compression machine for twenty minutes every ninety minutes. I'd always have to ask Alana to fill it up for me, and she hated that machine almost as much as I did.

In my final All Blacks years, from 2016 to 2019, I was always willing. That Achilles injury was a huge setback, and coming back from that was a real grind. But I did come back. In 2017, I played in just about every All Blacks game, but that's when the media were at their worst.

As I said, even though I mostly ignore the media, you can't help but hear whispers. *He doesn't deserve his place. He should be dropped. What's he done to deserve being selected?* I blocked most of it out and just stayed focused on playing the best I could.

I remember once being at an event and encountering Colin Meads, one of New Zealand's greatest rugby players ever. He's so revered that everyone was trying to get a piece of him. I was too shy to go over and say hello, but he came over to me and said, 'I'm a big fan of yours, Sonny. I love the way you play, your physicality, your skills. Don't ever lose that approach.'

With all the negative media around at that time, those words really helped remind me I was bringing something different to the game – if my style of play was good enough for the most respected All Black to have ever played, I knew I was on the right track. It was a great confidence booster.

* * *

In a Test against Australia, I got a head knock in the first two minutes. Actually, I found out later I was briefly unconscious. The doctors watching that game in Sydney didn't come and check on me; they left me on the field. I actually played well in that game, too. (Johnny would have told me afterwards if I hadn't. We have this thing between us where he always gives me a frank and honest opinion – even if I don't always love hearing it.)

I couldn't even remember being knocked out, but after the game I had all these messages on my phone from Alana, my mum, my dad, Khoder. They were all angry that I hadn't been taken off the field. The footage from the game isn't pretty, and I am clearly disorientated and struggling to stand and walk straight. I can't remember much, but I do remember after the tackle telling myself, *Stand up, bro. Stand up.* I was wondering why I felt so tired. I had another seventy-odd minutes to play so had to pull myself together.

When we moved to New Zealand, I found the media there much worse than in Australia. It was very strange to me, because Sonny's a New Zealander, so I wondered why they wouldn't support him, be proud of him. This was a man who had done his country proud in rugby league and rugby union, and he was also a decent, caring human who always tried to give back.

But everywhere Sonny went in the country, people only showed him love. From seven- to seventy-year-olds, boys, girls, women, men – they loved Sonny Bill. It's because he's such a genuine person, and he is always willing to be photographed, to stop to talk and listen to people. They appreciated that. They were delighted he was approachable and a very nice, respectful person. I am very proud of my husband and very angry at those harsh critics who refused to admit they were wrong and who never failed to have a dig, whether in newspapers or on TV. What annoyed me the most was that Sonny never had a right of reply. He just had to suck it up and get on with it.

I remember that Test match against the Wallabies. After Sonny set up a try and played really well, Phil Kearns, the former Wallabies captain who won two World Cups said:

'This is the same bloke that the New Zealand media said was past it. The same bloke who made a world-record twenty-six tackles against the Springboks two weeks ago.' Was that a headline in his own country? No, it wasn't.

In that same Test, when he got that heavy head knock that turned out afterwards to have caused a concussion, he continued to play despite his dizziness. So many times Sonny's talent and dedication to win was ignored. – Alana Williams

The mainstream media always seemed to downplay my abilities and say I was not worthy of the black jersey. But, conversely, in the Pasifika and Māori community and media, I was always held in high esteem, which I will always be proud of. More than 50 per cent of players in general are of Pasifika or Māori background, yet this is not translated in their representation in New Zealand's rugby media and commentators. Sometimes you find people in prominent positions and you wonder how they got there. This thought seems to pass my mind more and more, regardless of whatever field I am in.

In my experience, usually the harshest critics are the ones who have the least credentials, so who should I take seriously? The voice of someone who has never played at the highest level? Or the words of someone who has the respect of the rugby-playing world, like Colin Meads or Phil Kearns? I will go with Colin or Phil every time.

We went on tour and played France, Wales and Scotland. I had built a solid combination with Ryan Crotty, a very underrated player whom the media called a journeyman. Crotts was a whole lot better than that; he was a player you could depend on who made very few mistakes. I could close my eyes and pop a pass knowing he'd be right there.

In the France game, I was up against Mathieu Bastareaud, a hard-running massive ball of muscle. Playing against him was exactly the kind of challenge I relished, and I went at it. I had always wanted to play with the All Blacks against France, in France. Now I was on the field.

Doing the haka before that game, I was pumped and ready to go. The French revere the All Blacks, but of course they cheer on their own team like tens of thousands of people gone temporarily mad. Later, when you see those same screaming fans sitting in restaurants, calm and composed, it is like you're looking at different people.

I had a really strong, solid game that night. The French fans cheered rather than jeered me. Whenever I played in Europe the fans gave me big love, I think because they appreciate someone who plays with passion. Their media treated me in a very special way too, as if I was one of their own.

But I did have a moment of reverting to my league days by knocking the ball out with my hands in the dead ball area. It got me a yellow card and France were awarded a penalty try. I knew I had stuffed up. In league you can knock the ball out, but not in rugby. It was an honest mistake in the rush of play, but later I was hammered for it and TVNZ's *Breakfast* host Jack Tame was right when he predicted that this one moment was going to enable the haters. It sure did. Some in the media called it inexcusable. I made sure I reread the rulebook. After a ten-minute sin-binning, I came back on and we won the game 38–18.

The next week we played Scotland, and everyone was predicting we'd thrash them. As All Blacks, we always put pressure on ourselves not just to win, but to perform well. Scotland had beaten the Wallabies not long before, so we knew this wouldn't be an easy game. It turned out to be real close, but none of us had come at the game with the attitude they were easybeats. No-one is. You have to respect the opposition no matter who they are. And I probably had my stand-out game of the year. Everything flowed; my little grubber kicks, the offloads, the hard tackling, all the little unseen things. It just came together.

Next we were playing Wales on their famous Cardiff Arms Park home ground. That is always hard. We had a cracker and won by a good margin.

* * *

By the end of 2017, I was feeling confident in my form, having worked my way back from the Achilles injury and receiving a team award for Players' Player. I know this doesn't mean much to most people, but to me, being acknowledged by my teammates is the greatest recognition.

Back home in Christchurch in 2018 with the All Blacks, we were doing a tackling drill when who should come flying at me and chop me low but my good mate Ofa Tu'ungafasi. I stood up and my bad knee had locked. I could hardly stand. I knew straight away this was not good.

When you've had knee injuries like mine, excess bone grows to cope with the trauma. And if any player was to give you trauma it was Ofa, one of the strongest players I've played with (although I would never tell him that!). I love my brother Ofa, and we have a strong bond. There was no ill will in that tackle. As soon as I realised my knee was stuffed, I was back in that dark mental space called injury. After surgery, the surgeon advised my best rehab was to get on the gym bike. I spoke to the All Blacks physio, Pete Gallagher, a great guy who thinks outside the box. His advice for the same knee in 2015 had been unorthodox. He told me I'd lost flexion, which basically means the ability to bend an arm or a leg, so he suggested that every day he sit on my leg to straighten it.

Within a week it was straightened, and within two weeks I was running normally. Prior to that, my whole body mechanics had gone into adjusting to compensate for the wonky knee. Pete's method changed everything; I felt like an athlete again.

So, of course I listened to him again. I got on the bike, and then Pete suggested I do a little bit of running. Brodie Retallick was coming back from an injury, too, and Pete suggested we train together. I hadn't run for two or three weeks, and Brodie is known for being a fitness man. I was running hard and the big man was fifteen or twenty metres in front of me. But I was in it for the long haul, and I was going to focus on beating Brodie.

I'd do another session with Pete, and I'd feel about 40 per cent better. I got back into my old habit of doing the extras. I'd always had this mentality that if you do the extra work, you will always be a little bit ahead of the others.

The next session I was another 40 per cent better. I started to see light at the end of the tunnel then. Brodie was no longer outrunning me. I told Pete I thought I was ready to go back to full training. I felt good. Actually, I felt better than good, as I was so relieved to be back to normal.

I had another week of hard training and then the starting team was named early the next week. Number 12, Sonny Bill Williams. Good old Shag Hansen had shown faith in me, when only a few weeks back I'd had no faith in myself. I thought I'd never recover in time.

That's one thing about Steve Hansen: he's not afraid to pull the trigger from time to time. For instance, look at Rieko Ioane getting his first chance against the Lions, or Julian Savea, and look how easily they stepped up to the level expected. All they needed was their shot, and Steve gave it to them with no hesitation.

So, next up we were playing France, and I was playing really well. Their number 12, Wesley Fofana, runs a short ball, and I'm thinking, *It's time to light him up!* I *love* when the opposition tries to hit a hole that's suddenly no longer there. Instead, I was flying at him. But my timing was out.

It was one of those unlucky situations. I hit him at the top of the shoulder just as he bent forwards. I popped my AC joint out and fractured all the little bones in my left shoulder.

That was the end of the season for me. I was out for a long time after that. I headed home. Alana was pregnant with Zaid and he was born a couple of weeks later. At least I was there for the birth. Alhamdulillah!

***

Although I had been out with injury for much of the 2018 Super Rugby season, I had worked tirelessly and got my body right so I could be involved in the end-of-year tour. But then, in the second game of the tour versus England, injury struck again. Although I was out for the rest of the 2018 end-of-year tour, I still had a whole off-season to get myself ready for the goal of making the 2019 World Cup squad. And the big upside was, it wasn't my knee! It was my shoulder.

This time, instead of injury throwing me down the deep well of depression, I had this mad sense of gratitude. I knew I had the strength to get back up one more time and not only heal, but become a better person in the process, getting closer to my Creator. It was a mindset that enabled me to grind it out, stay patient, take the long view and work towards being an even better teammate, husband and father.

I had a really good 2019 off-season from a training perspective. We had Phil Healey, our old trainer from the Chiefs, and Rieko Ioane and I were training together. Once we finished, I had achieved some really good markers. I was the fastest, the strongest and the fittest I'd been in several years.

I was training with the Auckland Blues, then Rieko and I would go off and train together. When Rieko Ioane is beating you by ten metres in sprints every day and the gap slowly closes, that feels like a win, confirmation of my fitness and steady improvement. That dark hole was way behind me. I went into the 2019 Super Rugby season with the Blues on a high. I felt I was going to finish off my All Blacks career at the top and was looking forward to getting to play with my old mates one last time. I was named as vice-captain then captain of the Blues, and was feeling really good out there on the field.

We played the Stormers at Eden Park. I came off the bench, made a break straight away, feeling good. We won the scrum, I ran a short ball, hit a hole and set up a try with an offload to Otere Black, who scored under the posts.

But in the tackle my knee hit the ground hard; I got up and I knew something wasn't right. I felt sick: it was the same old feeling of trying to walk back to position but knowing my knee was shot. I'd done the cartilage and I'd only been on the field ten or fifteen minutes.

Back in the sheds, the boys were asking, 'You all right?' 'You okay?'

Right then, I went into that mindset of determination to work hard and get it right. I told myself, *Just this last season, Sonny.*

I had to wait for the usual medical investigations, and I was at home when the Blues doctor called me. I had started the season in really good nick – physically, I'd been hitting markers I hadn't hit for years. Then, bang.

There goes my knee again. I knew this was serious. After some scans, the Auckland Blues doctor had bad news. 'This could be it,' he told me. 'This injury could be the one you don't come back from.' I acted all tough and said, 'Okay, cool.' Then I just sat there and got really emotional, eyes all watery; I didn't know my wife could hear, but she was standing the other side of the door, listening to the call. It was hard for Alana to watch.

After the Achilles, Sonny got injury after injury. I was at the game in Auckland and he was playing amazingly well, just flying. I was feeling so happy for him. Then his knee goes.

When he got the not-so-good news about the MRI scan, I walked out to the backyard and found him crying. Going to the World Cup meant so much to him.

I didn't really have any words to console him, and of course I was crying. I said to him, 'This isn't the end. It isn't going to finish like this.' I see it as my duty to be a mirror Sonny can look into and see the best version of himself and hear only positive messages coming back. Usually it doesn't take him long to get over things.

He called Khoder and they talked things through. They decided to call a meeting with the doctors and the physio from the All Blacks as well as the Blues physio and a surgeon to see if there was a rehab path he could take, checking on progress every week, or if it was better to have surgery.

> It seemed to me nearly everyone was against surgery, but
> Sonny called the shots and said, 'Nah, I'm doing it.' I felt as
> if everyone had given up on him except Sonny himself. He had
> surgery and then he went at the rehabilitation as only he can do.
> That's Sonny. Every time he comes under extreme pressure, he
> finds a way to rise to the occasion. — Alana Williams

I was blessed to have Alana's support, and I was backing myself to get my knee strong enough to play at a high-enough level to make it into the World Cup squad. That old determination came back to me and so did the Islamic teachings of always being grateful for what you have. Rehab is no fun, but I had that goal and I pushed hard, did what the surgeon said, did what the physios said, and did what I had always done and stepped it up whenever I could. That year I played only the first and last games of the season for the Blues; that's how long it took to rehab back to form.

I got my body back to fitness levels that allowed me to play in the last game against the Hurricanes. Although I came off the field thinking I'd played well, I was pretty sure the powers that be would want me to play some park football to test out my fitness and boost my confidence levels, like they had done with Kieran Read. To my great surprise, that wasn't the case. I was handed the number 12 All Blacks jersey to play our next game against our greatest rival, South Africa.

ALL BLACKS v SPRINGBOKS:
SONNY BILL WILLIAMS MAGIC SAVES A HORROR SHOW

I played for fifty-eight minutes of that game, which ended up a 16–16 draw. I thought I had done my teammates and the black jersey proud. I was pleased with how my body performed and my skills were match fit. The headline that New Zealand media outlet Stuff ran suggested they felt the same. But Steve Hansen was obviously not impressed because I was called into a coaches' meeting with him, Ian Foster and Grant Fox. It was the first time I had ever been called out like that. Steve asked me to sit down and then told me that if they announced the 2019 All Blacks World Cup squad later that day, I would not be on the list. They carried on talking, but I wasn't hearing anything. All I could think was, *Why was I picked for that last game?* I'd gone from being in the starting fifteen to being told I would not even be named in the squad of thirty-two, all from that last performance? If I was to be omitted from the World Cup on how I played in that last game, I knew I'd done my best and I could definitely hold my head up high. But I was disappointed at how it was handled and thought Shag could have talked to me alone. I had played over fifty Tests and thought I deserved a little more respect than that. I guess he thought he needed Fox and Foster's support, but it didn't sit right with me.

I started thinking, *Couldn't you have asked me to coffee and been a bit more respectful about telling me how you felt? All of a sudden, I'm only good enough to play club rugby?* It was done in such an abrupt manner and I told myself it was just business. Not a relationship, not a bond between a player and his coaches. Just business. You are only necessary as long as you are useful. I know it happens to most players. One minute on top of the world, the next hurled off into outer space. It is brutal.

I was heading back to club rugby. But first, I had a frank talk with the coaches and told them exactly what I thought, how I felt the situation could have been managed in a better way. I explained that I knew it wasn't about me the individual, it was about the team, but they'd handled it wrong.

* * *

Park footy means lots of travel and playing in small towns in front of passionate crowds, often in pouring rain, and there is something about it that gets lost in the higher echelons of the game. They play with a freedom and happiness that is hard to find in those upper levels. It was good for me and reminded me what footy should feel like. Although I never openly expressed it at the time, deep down I was 100 per cent sure my All Blacks career was over.

Fast-forward a couple of weeks and the All Blacks were beaten by the Wallabies in Perth. They were getting savaged by the media. It was all doom and gloom, and commentators were predicting that we may lose the beloved Bledisloe for the first time in nearly twenty years. I was hurting for my brothers and sent messages of support to a few of the boys.

Then out of nowhere, I got a call from Shag.

'You're back in the team, Sonny.'

Just like that I was back training with the boys, and they were happy to see me. We were all pumped and ready to go. There is nothing more dangerous than a wounded All Blacks team. They named the team on the Tuesday before the game, and I was in the starting line-up. It was the biggest game of the year for the All Blacks, and I'd gone from being one of them to a club player and then back to the starting All Blacks squad in the blink of an eye. You'd never read about it – because it ain't meant to happen that way. Once you're dropped, you're supposed to be out of sight and out of mind.

We went to Auckland to play the Wallabies, who were on a high and pretty confident they knew how to beat us – and easily. Their number 12, Samu Kerevi, had an unbelievable game in that Perth outing, very physical.

NOT READY TO STOP . . . YET

I watched the game live and also in a replay. The whole time I was thinking, *Just give me a chance, because this is the type of battle I will thrive in.*

This was my shot, and I knew it was up to me. And I prepared as if it was my last game for the All Blacks ever, which it well could have been. As I always did, I prepared physically and mentally, but this time with even more intent. The game couldn't come quick enough.

The Aussie media were savage, with one headline on the back page of a Sydney paper reading, 'THE OLD BLACKS'. The headline was accompanied by a team photo, which the newspaper had altered with an app to age us and captioned with the words 'senior citizens'. I was the oldest in that team and I am pretty sure I won't look like that when I am an old man (though I wouldn't mind being that fit-looking at sixty!). It was a laugh for the boys and not too smart to try and rile us up. Disrespectful media like that can sting but it just adds another level of motivation for me.

We drove up to the stadium in our team bus and I remember getting off and thinking, *This is it.* In the changing room, I walked over to my jersey, which was hanging up ready, and got my boots out (I never, ever forgot them again after that first time!). The boys were all walking around or doing their own last-minute prep. I watched Ardie Savea and Rieko Ioane do their little dance moves. Big Sammy Whitelock had his head down, concentrating. Dane Coles, one of the players I respected the most in the squad and who I believed had the complete skill set that could have seen him play rugby league at the highest level, was putting on his boots. Captain Kieran 'Reado' Read moved around having a quick last word with all the players. I took it all in. I'm thinking, *I'm coming. I'm coming.*

Then we ran outside. It was raining and I thought the rain would impact my offload because of the slippery ball and the different tactics required to play in the wet. But I was too pumped to let that thought linger. I was just looking over at the Wallabies, picking out Kerevi who I considered one of the best centres in the world, and thinking, *Yeah, I'm coming for you.* A player with his talent needed my undivided attention.

I remember the day before I'd told my wife and Khoder, my family, that I was going to go out there and play hard and have fun. A steely resolve settled on us all.

I flew out of the line intent on making my presence felt from the off. But Kurtley Beale, world-class player that he is, outsmarted me and skip-passed to his outside man. Okay, but the start whistle had only just blown. I was in hunting mode. Made my tackles, and tried to be as physical as I could be, with or without the ball. We had to win to keep the Bledisloe Cup. And we did!

I love those big moments. We kept Kerevi quiet, and I played really well. I scored my twelfth try in fifty-three Tests and was part of a fierce team who beat the Wallabies 36–0. We received a standing ovation after the game and that is a mad buzz.

* * *

After that game against Australia, it was a great feeling in the sheds. I was proud of our resilience and how as a team we'd come through the struggles to put on such a dominant display.

Four weeks later, when they named the Rugby World Cup squad on the radio, I was at home with Alana and the kids, and Johnny was there too. Was I nervous? If it was purely based on my recent performances on the park against South Africa and Australia (not to forget my history in the black jersey), I felt like my name would be on the list. Despite the one conversation I had with the coaches, I knew my journey in 2011, 2015 and into 2019 meant I would be an asset to the team. I was no longer the shy, unconfident, mixed Sāmoan-Australian boy who had a 'yes sir, no sir' attitude to authority, whether they be right or wrong. I was now a proud, confident Pasifika man who knew he had earned his position in the squad. When the list was read out, my name was there. Alana was crying, Johnny was crying. I had very mixed feelings as I was happy to be going to defend the title and play in my third World Cup but I was also very disappointed for my good mate Owen Franks, one of our greatest ever props, and fellow Pacific brother Ngani Laumape – another former league player with whom I had a special rapport – who didn't make the squad. That made me feel a bit empty instead of full of all the joys. Two guys I was close to would not be joining us. That could have been me.

I'd been elevated back up, from club to elite and was in my third All Blacks Rugby World Cup squad. All the work, self-belief and heart had paid off. I look back to that young fella who arrived in Sydney with some talent but so much self-doubt and I am really aware of the way I have been able to shape my life. Key to all that was my belief in Islam; Islam helped me learn how to leave my torments behind. I was so grateful to be doing what I loved, living my life as a professional sportsman, and now I was united with my All Blacks teammates in wanting to make history. I knew that 2019 was going to be my last year in the All Blacks and I wanted to finish on a high note.

2019 Rugby World Cup Squad

Forwards: Ardie Savea, Sam Cane, Matt Todd, Luke Jacobson, Scott Barrett, Sam Whitelock, Brodie Retallick, Patrick Tuipulotu,

Nepo Laulala, Angus Ta'avao, Ofa Tu'ungafasi, Joe Moody,
Atu Moli, Dane Coles, Codie Taylor, Liam Coltman,
Kieran Read (c.)
Backs: Jordie Barrett, Ben Smith, Sevu Reece, George Bridge,
Rieko Ioane, Jack Goodhue, Anton Lienert-Brown, Ryan Crotty,
Sonny Bill Williams, Beauden Barrett, Richie Mo'unga,
Aaron Smith, TJ Perenara, Brad Weber

* * *

Imaan was turning five and this was her dad's last time in the
All Blacks, his third World Cup, and I was so glad I was there in
Japan to watch him. This was a huge achievement for Sonny after
his injuries. The way he got himself back to match fitness made
me proud. At thirty-four, he was the oldest in the team and was
on track to make history going after his third World Cup.

Things didn't go exactly as we all hoped. Losing the semi-
final against England was brutal. To keep Sonny off in that
game seemed a mistake to me and not because I'm his wife.
They got beaten in the first half, yet they didn't go to the bench
at half-time. When they finally did, Sonny came on but it was
too late, there weren't enough minutes left. So, the All Blacks
came third.

Sonny had a magic that could change a game because he not
only had the skills and physicality, but he could also see it, the gaps,
where the play was headed: he could read the game. If I'm watching

a game on television with Sonny, he'll say, 'Why are they doing that move? It won't work.' He took that ability into every game he played.

At the end of that Bronze-medal match against Wales, Imaan got to go on the field with her dad, and she carried his medal around. When we got back home to New Zealand, she took the medal to school; she was so happy and proud.

I think when Sonny's an old man he can look at those photos of him and Imaan on the field in Tokyo and be reminded of the importance of family and our cherished memories. – Alana Williams

It wasn't to be. We travelled to Japan looking to claim another World Cup, and after finishing top of the table in our pool we were ready to face Ireland in the quarter-final. I was on the bench for the start of that game, and, without disrespecting Ireland, it was a good feeling to beat them 46–14 and set ourselves up to play England in the semi-final. We were going in as reigning champions and, after beating our rivals South Africa in the Pool B match to get there, we were probably going in favourites. But nothing is ever certain on a footy field and England had a steely resolve that was evident as we performed the haka. They had a point to prove and they hit hard from the opening whistle. They did everything you have to do to win. At the end of eighty minutes, we were beaten by the better team, and as much as it always hurts to lose, they deserved the 19–7 win because they never let up. As our All Blacks captain, Kieran Read, said after the game, 'We gave our all, gave it everything we had, but just came up short. We're all hurting.' Steve Hansen backed him up, saying, 'There's no shame in it, but a lot of hurt which could all feed into a lot of All Blacks teams in the future.'

Like I have said before, there is nothing more dangerous than a wounded All Blacks team and that fire to win and reclaim that Cup will smoulder until 2023, when I have no doubt that it will ignite. But after the game, we all needed bulletproof vests when we sat down together to analyse what went wrong. It was a grim conversation, as the coaches pulled no punches, and the team had their say. Then we just had to get on with it.

That hurt fuelled us in the third-place match against Wales. We won that game 40–17. We hadn't come to win bronze. We wanted the gold medal and I wanted to lift the trophy for the third time, so I had some struggles in my head with that disappointment. But I played well in that game and did what I always want to do when I wear the All Blacks jersey: honour my brothers who have come before and build on a tradition for those who will follow. After fifty-eight Test matches, I don't care what my critics say: I gave all I could to that team and was very proud to represent New Zealand.

In an interview after the game, I said that while obviously it was hard to lose, there are more important things in life, and I wasn't going to sit and sulk over something that's not going to bring me happiness. I copped some flak over those comments; I think they wanted me to be crying in a corner. But I have learned that sport is only ever one part of a sportsperson's life, and it is not the only purpose. Sure, I go out to win. But if I play well, and give it my all, that is all I can do. Having my daughter with me on the field after the game against Wales, to sit and soak up the moment, and reflect on what it took to be there, was a beautiful thing. I was so thankful to New Zealand rugby, who had given me the opportunity to play those fifty-eight Test matches and also allowed me to keep boxing and to play rugby sevens. To play for the last time in the All Blacks jersey was emotional but I am forever part of rugby history and when I am an old man I will have lots of stories about the games we played and the people we played against. Alhamdulillah, I am so grateful for it all.

Do I wish we had won? Yes. But sometimes the Most High has other plans.

CHAPTER 14

Being where my feet are

After the World Cup, I had to think about what I wanted to do and how my body was holding up. Before that, I had told Khoder he could have conversations exploring other opportunities, but my focus had to be on the All Blacks and honouring that jersey, so I didn't want to discuss the future or know what offers were coming in. In the last few years, I really have tried to live by the saying: 'I try to be where my feet are.' Once I was back in New Zealand and Alana and I talked about it, I knew I was not ready to retire. At that point I thought I would stay in New Zealand and play another year of club rugby. Meanwhile, Khoder was sorting through offers and possibilities and he presented some to me for us to discuss. I decided the offer to join the Toronto Wolfpack, who were playing in the British Super League and based in the UK, was too good to turn down. Sure, the money was great, but the opportunity to return to playing rugby league and be part of the Super League was also a big lure. To transition back to league would be a challenge, but I am a sportsman and I need to have something to aim for. Importantly, that goal has to be worthy of all the sacrifices I ask my family to make to enable me to continue to play elite sport.

Talking to Toronto coach Brian McDermott and hearing his vision for Toronto in the Super League gave me a new sense of purpose. The aim was to succeed. And the fact that Toronto is a multicultural city and that I might help open up the North American market was another factor. I know what sport did for me as a youngster. If I can help young fellas find opportunities they may not have had otherwise, then I would be very happy. And Toronto wanted me not just as a player but for a leadership role; they wanted me to mentor the younger players and help where I was needed. It was a new challenge, and the challenge is always important to me. I want to push myself, stretch my skills and be a better player and a better person, and joining the Wolfpack ticked all those boxes. We wanted to win the northern hemisphere's premier rugby league competition in 2020. I was on board for that.

The team was based in Manchester, so it meant a move for Alana and the kids. That was a hard wrench for Alana, as while the details were getting sorted, she was pregnant with our fourth child. Dealing with three kids, a pregnancy (and hers have not been easy) and the thought of moving countries was a lot of pressure on both of us.

> Sonny was in Britain for six weeks. He came home two days before our son Essa was born. We thought the upheaval was over when we were all in the UK together, but one week later, everything went into Covid lockdown. – Alana Williams

It was an awful time for so many, and though we didn't know how bad things would get around the world, we all felt worried about what was to come. But Alana and I gave thanks to Allah that she hadn't waited to travel because if she had, the borders would have been closed and the kids and Alana would have been stuck in New Zealand and I would have been in Manchester without them.

As Alana said, within the first week of her and the kids arriving, the whole country was placed in lockdown and we had no idea how long that would be for. At first, it was full-on hectic with jet lag and a new environment. Alana and I pretty soon realised that with four kids in the house and limited outside interaction we had to put some structure in place, for all of us. We were home-schooling the older kids and so having activities at certain times of the day really helped to keep them on track. We were allowed to leave the house to exercise as a family and we were lucky as within the ten-kilometre radius that limited travel we had farmland and forest to explore. We went walking every day and it was lovely to be with the kids, checking out the natural world. Though the day Zaid and I were chased by cows is not the interaction with nature I was wanting to teach him about. I didn't know cows could run so fast. It was pretty funny! As tough as the pandemic has been for so many around the world, and my heart goes out to them, the world slowing down saw me able to spend uninterrupted time with my family. This has seen us flourish and has strengthened our bond. I just enjoyed being with them. Alana loved it too, because it was just us.

But I never forgot what I was there for, so my training never stopped. That was always part of my day. Weights, boxing, bike, yoga, stretching, running – everything I could do to maintain my fitness I did, always hoping that things would get better.

That wasn't to be and after five months, I was stuck in limbo, not able to play and not sure what to do. And that's when discussions with the Roosters began. The NRL allowed me to return to Australia. Packing up again was not quite as hard because we had barely unpacked, and the thought of being back in Australia brought comfort to Alana and me, though I think Alana would have liked to go back to New Zealand. So, we packed up the kids and committed to the two weeks' quarantine required to make a return to the NRL possible. The challenge of that and connecting with the Roosters boys lit me up.

I was pretty fit despite not being able to train with teammates for five months and before I flew back I had another clean-out of my knee to be sure it would hold up. I can't even remember how many general anaesthetics I have had, but it is a lot! I was looking forward to getting back on a field with the team and I was ready for another stint in the NRL. Especially after two weeks in hotel quarantine with the kids!

My first game was against the Canberra Raiders, and I came in off the bench in the second half. I loved being back out there, playing the game I grew up playing. I expected to be pushed, and I was. The rule changes to the game made it a lot faster, but nothing I couldn't adapt to. Post-quarantine, I still had to work on my fitness, but coming away with the 18–6 win was awesome. I played in the next three games then missed the qualifying final because of an injury to my neck, but I made it back for the do-or-die semi-final. We lost the match 22–18 to the Canberra Raiders, but the boys had given it their all to claw back to a near-win when it was looking bad early on.

We almost got there. I felt bad for the boys, but experience has shown that sometimes the fairytale doesn't happen. That is a hard lesson to learn but sometimes your best effort doesn't bring home the trophy. I had a chat about how to deal with that with some of the younger boys and how they can use that disappointment to fuel their efforts next season and beyond.

> [Sonny Bill Williams] was fantastic tonight [in the semi-final]. He was a real success story this year. He came back and slowly got back to a situation where he could play. I thought he was big tonight. But he will be a success at whatever he does because he has the mindset and willpower. – Peter Sterling

> All those who bagged [Sonny Bill Williams] in the lead-up – he stood up like a champion. Not bad for 35 with little prep. If that's his last NRL game, it's been a great career. – Danny Weidler

After the game I was asked if that was it for me, and at that point I didn't know. I had to see what was happening with Toronto, but so much depended on the way Covid-19 was controlled and it wasn't looking good in the UK or the US. And I had to admit that my thirty-five-year-old joints were finding it a bit tougher to get out of the starting blocks each week. I was doing everything I could to keep my body competitive on a footy field, but the injuries had taken a toll. I worked hard to get back to an elite level and I was proud of that, but even after the extra effort I was putting in to be ready for game day, I still had to take too many painkillers and drugs just to play. At one point, I had been taking so many painkilling drugs I ended up with burning in my gut and had to have an endoscopy to check out what was happening.

In that last game against the Raiders, I had so many drugs in my system and yet I still had pain in my neck, back and knee. I came in after warm-up and asked the doc for more. He said he had a duty of care to uphold and that if I had any more, I could overdose. Although I still had the drive, I knew my time in footy had come to an end.

Not long after, I was doing a boxing interview and I just came out with the news that I was not going to play league or union anymore. Every player fears injury will be followed by a loss of form and being dropped. I had worked hard to keep bouncing back but Alana and I had talked about it and we feared me being forced out rather than going out on my own terms. I've had anxiety about injury, as you know, since I was first told by a doctor my career might be over by age twenty-three.

I'm proud to say that my last game of league in Australia was at the highest level, playing in an NRL semi-final. My last All Blacks game finished on a good note too. It was time to step away physically from the game. And I had other things I wanted to do, and new challenges waiting. Leaving the game physically was easier than I thought, but mentally the game still lingers. In the end, the conflict between what my body could give and what my mind expected was just too distant. Combine that with all the painkillers and anti-inflammatories and I knew I couldn't play footy at an elite level anymore. I was in constant pain and I never wanted to be there just to make up the numbers. I always wanted to add value my way.

I am forever grateful to my Creator for giving me such a long career. And I've been fortunate to have played alongside some exceptional sportspeople. There are so many players who have given me friendship over the years and countless others who made an impression. I've always shown respect to every man I ever took the field with in the different rugby codes, as well as the brothers I have met through boxing. I've already paid tribute to a few, but I want to thank all the teammates who I played with over the years for allowing me to achieve dreams I never thought possible. I hope you all know I will always be supporting you from afar.

CHAPTER 15

Finding my voice

I am a very different person from the man I once was. I used to worry about saying the wrong thing or giving an opinion because I didn't believe that what I had to say mattered or would make a difference. That's down to the insecurity and low self-esteem I talked about earlier. I am in a good place now because of my faith and my family. But I have also grown up a lot. I have matured and everything I have experienced up to this point on my life's journey has created the man I am today. A man at peace with it all because of Allah.

When I started to gather information and brush up on all things Sonny Bill, I found a video on YouTube titled 'Sonny Bill Williams: 4 moments of charity/respect/humility'.

The first clip shows a Tongan girl approaching Sonny Bill on the field requesting something. He follows her to the crowd, where a Tongan player hands Sonny his baby so he can take a photo. Sonny is entirely in that moment, acknowledging a fellow Polynesian, knowing how good it makes the father feel. He touches the man's arm and walks over to acknowledge his family and other Tongans. It is a simple but beautiful moment.

The second moment points out that Sonny Bill had offered free tickets to any Syrian refugees who wanted to go to the 2019 World Cup. He proactively reached out to do that.

The third is after the All Blacks beat the Springboks in the 2015 Rugby World Cup semi-final. An inconsolable Jesse Kriel, Sonny's admirable mid-field opponent, is down on his haunches in dismay. Sonny goes to him, bends down and embraces him. It's more than a quick hug; he embraces the South African as one rugby brother to another, saying in the nicest possible way, 'This was our day. Tomorrow will be yours.'

Then, as the rain pours down, he helps Kriel to his feet, talking to him, his face close to Kriel's. For my money, that moment could have been freeze-framed and shown around the world as a lesson in aroha, respect, shown by one special athlete to another special athlete. *We fought a good battle, now we are no longer enemies but, rather, the opposite. Friends of mutual respect.*

The fourth moment is the one I described in the introduction to this book: Sonny's astonishing gesture of, first, spontaneous concern when a fourteen-year-old fan was tackled by a security guard when he ran out onto the field after the All Blacks won the 2015 Rugby World Cup.

The rest is history. That boy's hero put an arm around him and walked him back to his parents in the stand. Then he removed his gold medal and put it around the boy's neck.

Those moments – and I know there are many more – show the real Sonny Bill Williams, the man. No opponent ever got the better of him on the field, and he is a legendary sportsman. But what elevates him in my eyes is his heart, his empathy and his willingness to speak out for those who can't speak out for themselves. That is the true greatness of SBW.

– Alan Duff

In May 2020, the world was confronted by the shocking death of George Floyd while in police custody. The spotlight was turned onto the racism that still lives too close to the surface of our lives. For people of colour, this was more than a moment of outrage; it was an acknowledgement and understanding of the different ways you are treated because of the colour of your skin. Alan Duff and I have talked about how America has treated its black sports stars historically. Win the world heavyweight championship like black American Joe Frazier did in 1970 and then see if you can withdraw $10,000 from your own bank account. The answer was no.

Muhammad Ali dared to challenge the white establishment. He refused to be drafted into the US Army for service in Vietnam, even when he was threatened with jail and warned his world heavyweight title would be stripped from him. He was hated for daring to speak up, but he wouldn't be silenced. Strong-willed, he snatched the narrative and never handed it back. For the world to change, for equality to be real, we need people to speak up.

I am learning to do that: to speak out when it matters, or when I see injustice. I am determined to honour my principles. (I mentioned earlier that, with the All Blacks' blessing, I covered up the logo of one of our sponsors, a bank, because Islam does not permit interest.) I don't care who it is; if you are being held back, held down, you have a right to push back and keep pushing until you are treated as an equal.

Sport – and sportspeople – can help shine that light into dark places. It can unite, inspire and free. Look at Jesse Owens, an African American who, in the 1936 Olympics held in Berlin, won four gold medals. His incredible achievement in front of Adolf Hitler powerfully dispelled the dangerous Nazi theory of Aryan superiority. He showed that a person of colour could win the day. There is a lesson in that. Or the spotlight placed on racism and segregation in America by Tommie Smith and John Carlos at the 1968 Mexico City Olympics, as they raised their arms straight up in the air, each with their hand in a black glove in a Black Power salute. Or the Australian man next to them on the podium, Peter Norman, who wore a badge in solidarity, calling for an end to racism.

Rugby gave me an international profile, allowing me to thrive on the world stage. The love and tributes I received on announcing my retirement – from fans, fellow players, opponents, governing bodies, referees and even the media – made me feel empowered to follow my path more boldly. But I am just a man – I hope a caring man, with a heart. I have my flaws, and I know what it is to struggle. I was blessed and I found the light and the right partner and so I am on the path to be the better person I have always yearned to be.

Nowadays, I feel I most represent Polynesian and Māori people, especially the youngsters who are unsure what the future holds. Not all kids come from a privileged background. Not all kids have it easy growing up and many have to worry if there's food on the table. It is too easy for these kids to be left behind.

It needs to be understood how colonisation has affected Pasifika and Māori people, just as it has affected Indigenous Australians. Losing your culture, your way of life, has a drastic effect on any race, and this intergenerational trauma can echo on for generations. It can be seen today in our higher crime rates, worse health statistics, higher suicide rates, poor education outcomes, low home ownership – the list goes on and on. I'm glad that New Zealanders in general have lately made a major shift towards understanding our Polynesian culture, our outlook. And good on the media for promoting that.

This is not a demand for an apology. It is a plea for awareness. Colonisation is not just a moment in history with no after-effects.

When I was with Alan Duff in Auckland early in June 2021, working on this book, we ran into a Māori friend, Rua Tipoki – a former top rugby player who didn't quite make it to the All Blacks – and another mate, Quade Cooper. We chatted about various things, and my Māori brother expressed pride in me having done so well in sport. That talk moved on to the importance of self-belief – or the impact a lack of it can have. He recalled how, growing up, he was told that Māori don't quite have it; didn't have the fire or the work ethic or the ability. If you hear that enough, you start to believe it. He spoke about brown people these days turning a corner and starting to believe in themselves.

There were four of us standing there that day: Quade Cooper, the former Wallaby; Alan Duff, who has gone from serving time in jail to having his books published around the world; our Māori bro, who led his Irish club side in a haka before playing the All Blacks and came close to a major upset; and me. We were four brown people who'd come from difficult backgrounds yet made it. This is what we all want for young Pasifika and Māori. Self-belief that grows into success.

Here's a little story that, on the face of it, seems to be about my dad. But it goes way beyond that – and way back before it, too.

After I retired, I had an offer to become a rugby league and rugby union commentator for the Nine and Stan networks. I was ready to take on that challenge, and though I knew I'd have a lot to learn, I was ready to step up and do it. When I told my old man, he said, 'But don't you have to be a rugby person to do that job?' I was shocked and a bit dirty. I was the winner of two Rugby World Cup medals, winner of a Super Rugby championship, I had won two NRL grand finals and had played over 300 professional games in both codes. Wasn't I a rugby person?

I reacted strongly, even angrily, but when I thought about it later, I realised my father was just expressing that colonised Sāmoan outlook of, *We are not good enough.* It was his instinctive reaction, and it said more about the world he had grown up in than what he thought about me.

That kind of attitude has long been indoctrinated in Pasifika and Māori people. Those years of being downtrodden have an effect on your psychology; you automatically think in the negative. My father was the product of several generations of oppression. So even when all the evidence says his son is more than qualified to commentate on a sport he's excelled at, he still struggles to believe it. That's what colonisation has done.

If you look at how many Polynesians and Māori play in league and union teams in Australia and New Zealand, and increasingly in the UK and France, and then look at the lack of representation at an administrative and management level, you can see the problem. It would be good to see more brown coaches, board members and CEOs come through. It is important for our young people that Māori and Pasifika people are represented in all levels of society, because you can't aspire to be what you can't see. It is like me back at school, thinking I couldn't do anything that required an education. My focus was sport, because I had seen brown footy players on TV. I could aspire to be one of them because they were like me.

There are so many things in the world that need to change, and I am realising more and more that it is up to people with a platform – people like me – to call out what is wrong. The only way we can open people's eyes to injustice is to talk about it.

When Australia and New Zealand established the trans-Tasman bubble at the end of May 2021, allowing people from both countries quarantine-free travel, I flew back to New Zealand and headed for Queenstown. I was travelling with former Socceroo and refugee advocate Craig Foster.

We wanted to shine a spotlight on Australia's shameful treatment of refugees and asylum seekers. For too long refugee policy has focused on the politics of securing votes rather than the humanitarian focus it should have. Too many asylum seekers are housed in dismal camps on Christmas Island and in Nauru and Papua New Guinea. In 2021 alone, there are about 240 human beings imprisoned in offshore detention centres and $800 million has been allocated to be spent keeping them there. And one family of four, with two Australian-born children – Nades, Priya, Kopika and Tharnicaa Murugappan – spent over three years detained on Christmas Island before they were brought back to the mainland because Tharnicaa required urgent medical attention. The Australian Government has spent an incredible $10 billion keeping asylum seekers like this family in camps like convicted criminals.

These are people who committed no crime. After fleeing oppression and war in their home countries, they had legally sought asylum. Instead of being welcomed, for eight years they've been stuck in limbo. And the government doesn't give a damn. People's views on refugees have always baffled me. It really hits my heart that they are treated with such contempt.

In 2015, I visited a Syrian refugee camp in Lebanon, and it really opened my eyes. The first question we should all ask ourselves is: *What is a refugee?* When people understand that a refugee is actually a person seeking refuge from persecution, fleeing from a war or a cruel regime run by a dictator's brutal police or military, or a person fleeing from a society that would imprison and kill them for political or religious views, it will hopefully make them think differently.

A refugee doesn't really want to leave their homeland – few people do. Home is home. These people have been forced to leave their homes.

Why wouldn't the Australian Government let them in? Australia has been made better by the contribution of displaced people and refugees and until 2001, we were a country that mostly addressed asylum seekers with compassion. If we allowed these people to settle, we would see the benefits more than the disadvantages.

Visiting that camp in Lebanon made me question humanity as a whole. It was a devastating place. I watched kids play, like kids do the world over, only the mud puddles they were splashing in was raw sewage. You look into the eyes of the parents in a place like that and all you see is hopelessness. Bitterness. The profound disappointment of people who are forgotten, ignored. I saw some older kids, aged thirteen to eighteen, who had set up real basic makeshift schools in tents. These were kids grateful to be alive after losing most of their family to war.

With the help of an interpreter, I spoke to kids who told me they wanted to go back to Syria and not just survive but thrive. 'We want to go back to Syria and be productive in society, rebuild our lives.' Hearing that really hit me. Again, as I said, few people *want* to leave their homeland. It is an act of sheer desperation. Now they were in limbo. They couldn't go back to Syria, but they weren't Lebanese citizens. The adults had no opportunity to work, and though there were those makeshift schools in the camp, the kids had no access to a proper education. Where is the light at the end of the tunnel for these people? The sad truth is, there isn't one. They have to move on and keep moving on, maybe even to Australia, in the hope of finding a peaceful place to settle where they might rebuild their shattered lives. This experience has given me a deeper sense of gratitude for all that my family and I have.

So, Craig and I were in New Zealand while the Australian Prime Minister was there, wanting to look the politicians in the eye and ask them: 'Why?' And also ask them: 'Where has all the money gone? Ten billion dollars!' The workers in the camps are on about $10 an hour.

So why does it cost $800 million to house 240 refugees? That's $3.33 million per person. And the camps are not the Hilton. It makes me angry, and I can't see how that amount of money can be accounted for. I think we all have a duty to get our priorities right along with giving ourselves a big dose of humanity, and then to call on the government to change its policies. Imagine it was you, having to get up, leave everything you've known, grab your kids and your family, everything you've worked for in your life and flee. All we want is for the government to treat people in a humane way and give them a fair go.

I'm grateful to be blessed with such an amazing brother who is also such a decent human being. He's not perfect – who is? – and he has never claimed to be. But he's never made the same mistake twice and always learned from those slip-ups.

I'm so proud he uses his public profile as a platform to help others, like going to Christchurch to comfort and show compassion for his fellow Muslims who survived that awful massacre in March 2019. This same man donated his $100,000 boxing purse to the Christchurch Earthquake Recovery Fund. He is speaking out on behalf of refugees kept in dismal camps in offshore Australia and Nauru. He's not running around the A-list celebrity circuit partying on big yachts, wining and dining in fancy places. He's out there fighting for people who fled intolerable conditions in their own country just wanting a better life in Australia. I am very proud of him. I love him heaps, even when he introduces me as 'Nail', not Niall. I wouldn't have him any other way. — Niall Williams

I was a late starter at watching my brother Sonny play footy. I didn't go to his games till I was a bit older and was sent to live in Sydney because I was wagging school in my rebellious phase. Dad said come over to live with me and my partner, promising he wouldn't be on my case.

Having two brothers there as well as my father meant I at least had family support and so I went. I saw my brothers as more my father figures; they let me know they had my back. While I was at a bit of a loose end, Sonny paid for my early childhood education diploma and offered to set me up with my own private centre. I declined because, like a lot of Polynesians, the thought of sitting exams and possibly failing was too daunting. I've been in early childhood education eight years now.

I started to become aware of how popular my brother was with the rugby league fans when I went to watch him play. Everyone cheered madly for him, and it made me feel so proud. When the media criticised him — which wasn't very often over in Australia — I'd get mad.

It was Sonny who kind of coached me how to handle him being criticised. He'd say, 'They don't know us. Who cares about people we've never even met?' As I said, I was a late starter to the SBW fan club but naturally I became a pretty avid one.

When he was leaving the Bulldogs, he took us family members aside to tell us. We were shocked, couldn't believe it. Dad was very upset; he just didn't understand it. I cried and we hugged, and he was off to France.

But he never ever forgot his family; he paid for me to go to Toulon, to Japan. Back to France. Paid mega dollars to get me from Sydney to Auckland because it was Christmas and last-minute fares were through the roof. He just wanted me home with Mum for Christmas; cost didn't come into it. Words can't express how I feel about him.

We live just twenty minutes away from Sonny in Sydney now. Dad and his partner live close by too. He loves my kids and my daughter, named after my sister, Niall, just adores him. She converted to Islam because of him. And there was no pressure from either me or Sonny. It was what she wanted.

I actually had no idea how big rugby league was in Australia. Or how big the All Blacks are in New Zealand – even their international opponents have huge respect for them. My brother a top league player, a Kiwi and then in the All Blacks?

I always watch his and Niall's games. And I kept the Bulldogs as my favourite league team even though he left them. If he's not playing for the ABs, I don't watch.

When he offered to put up the money for me to get my own childcare centre, I didn't have the confidence to do the extra study required. Johnny and I called ourselves the 'black sheep' of the family. But we turned out all right.

When I had a miscarriage, he flew Mum straight over to Sydney. He's helped us all out. In private, he's a goof. We've got videos of him dancing and doing silly, crazy things. He gets everyone involved. His body might have gotten a bit old, but his humour hasn't aged one day.

No matter how much pain he was in, how tired he was after a hard game, he always had time for us. I'm proud to talk about him. Proud to be the sister of such an exceptional, special man.

– Denise Williams

* * *

I've come so far from that teenager who couldn't speak up. Now I am using my voice to speak about injustice and also using my voice in a new career. My next challenge is as a sports commentator for the Nine Network in Australia and for Stan Sport. I am a big believer that without challenges, there is no growth, so pushing myself into this new space made sense. Sure, I could have just retired and led a quiet, comfortable life, but I am not one to sit back and let life go by. Is it daunting? Yes. Is it a little overwhelming? Yes. But that is what makes it interesting.

And, as I said earlier, over here in Australia there's no Islander representation in the media, at board level, as CEOs or sporting coaches. Islanders make up about 50 per cent of league and rugby teams, but zero per cent of the management jobs. I'd like to think I got the commentating role because I have runs on the board as a professional league and rugby player. I know both sports, but there are lots of Kiwi and Islander players like me; why haven't they found a place? It feels wrong that someone with my résumé should feel uncomfortable being in his own environment. It feels wrong that I should be invited to some official after-match function and look around to see I'm the only brown person in the room. So, I am really pleased and proud that Channel Nine has contracted me to their commentary team. I'm still waiting for the other channels to employ Pacific Islanders with proven sports records. There are heaps of them out there. Pasifika people need to see themselves represented in all aspects of society. They need their stories, their culture and their language to be treated equally in Australia and New Zealand. I am glad that is starting to happen.

As we worked on this book, Alan Duff and I talked about the incredible heritage of the Polynesian people. At least 5000 years ago – perhaps even 10,000 – our seafaring ancestors made their way from Taiwan, navigating by the stars to eventually settle every island in the Pacific Ocean. That strength, ingenuity and resilience is something all young Pasifika people should know runs in their blood. It shows that they are capable of anything they set their minds to and work hard for.

A French journalist, Karim Ben Ismail, once said about me, 'You can't stop the sun from shining.' While he might have meant it as an offhand remark, it stuck with me: not because it was about me, but because it is true. No matter what happens on the field, in the ring or in my life, it is a reminder that Allah does not burden a soul beyond what they can bear. It's a reminder to push through and keep going, keep trying, because the sun will keep shining and a new day will come.

If my story shows anything, it is that hard work and focus can make a difference. I hope I can encourage others to back themselves and be brave enough to walk through those doors. What matters most to me now is faith, family, friends and helping to point out injustice in the world. I have been given a gift and a profile, and I have to use them to make a difference. And I still love my sport!

I feel blessed. All those years ago, my one dream was to buy my mum her own house with that fancy wallpaper. I am proud that I did that and she has lived in that home for many years. My mum says she thanks her lucky stars for how life turned out. And so do I. Without the loving, supportive, inspiring figures like my mum and my nan, without the lessons I have learned from my father, without my brother and my sisters, without my wife and four beautiful children, I would not be the man I am today. I thank Allah for it all.

SBW: the Stats

RUGBY LEAGUE

Club Career	Years	Played	T	G	FG	Pts
Canterbury-Bankstown Bulldogs	2004–08	73	31	0	0	124
Sydney Roosters	2013–14, 2020	50	11	0	0	44
Toronto Wolfpack	2020	5	0	0	0	0
Total		128	42	0	0	168

Other Club Games	Years	Played	T	G	FG	Pts
World Club Challenge	2005, 2014	2	0	0	0	0
Total Club Games		130	42	0	0	168

Test Matches	Years	Played	T	G	FG	Pts
New Zealand	2004, 2006–08, 2013	12	5	0	0	20

TOTAL CAREER GAMES	2004–08, 2013–14, 2020	142	47	0	0	188

SONNY BILL WILLIAMS

RUGBY UNION

Club Career	Years	Played	T	G	Conv	FG	Pts
Toulon	2008–10	33	6	0	0	0	30
Canterbury	2010–11	7	4	0	0	0	20
Crusaders	2011	15	5	0	0	0	25
Chiefs	2012–15	29	6	0	0	0	30
Panasonic Wild Knights	2012	7	2	0	0	0	10
Counties Manukau	2014, 2019	3	0	0	0	0	0
Auckland Blues	2017–19	17	0	0	0	0	0
Total		111	23	0	0	0	115

Test Matches	Years	Played	T	G	Conv	FG	Pts
New Zealand	2010–19	58	13	0	0	0	65

	Years	Played	T	G	Conv	FG	Pts
TOTAL CAREER GAMES	2008–15, 2017–19	169	36	0	0	0	180

RUGBY SEVENS

New Zealand	2016

BOXING CAREER

Date	Opponent	Result	W	D	L
27/05/2009	Gary Gurr	Won – TKO	1	0	0
30/06/2010	Ryan Hogan	Won – TKO	2	0	0
29/01/2011	Scott Lewis	Won – UD	3	0	0
5/06/2011	Alipate Liava'a	Won – UD	4	0	0
8/02/2012	Clarence Tillman	Won – TKO	5	0	0
8/02/2013	Francois Botha	Won – UD	6	0	0
31/01/2015	Chauncy Welliver	Won – UD	7	0	0
26/06/2021	Waikato Falefehi	Won – UD	8	0	0

Acknowledgements

Acknowledgements from Alan Duff

Thanks to Khoder Nasser for being so supportive and insightful. Thanks to Vanessa Radnidge for her tireless work and undying enthusiasm. Thanks to Jenny Rogers and the team at Transcription Services. Biggest thanks to Sonny Bill for sharing his story with us.

Acknowledgements from Sonny Bill

I would like to thank Alan Duff for helping me to tell my story. It was an honour to work with this Māori man to tell it the right way. And thank you to Mona Seiuli for the wonderful front cover photo.

Thank you to Vanessa Radnidge and the Hachette Australia, Hachette Aotearoa New Zealand and Hodder UK teams who have worked so hard to create this book with me. And thank you to all the hardworking booksellers who are helping to share my story.

For me to achieve my goals and aspirations while overcoming the doubts that once seemed all encompassing, the Most High has put many good people in my path and I would like to thank some of those special people here.

My love of sport was derived from my father's toughness and unrelenting desire to see his children succeed and reach heights he never did. I now know that he pushed us because he saw the God-given talent we possessed, even before we did.

Thanks to . . .

The special teachers who recognised my talent from a young age and pushed me in the right direction: Mr Waller and Mr Phillips from Owairaka District School, Mr Ball from Wesley Intermediate and Ms Mita from Mount Albert Grammar School.

The footy coaches throughout my childhood, whose support and encouragement will never be forgotten: Adolf Guttenbeil, Sheral and Julian Cameron, Tillam Kapsin. And, though they never coached me, if it wasn't for the commitment of the Lipscombe family to our small rugby league and athletics clubs, led by Ross and Anne, I and many other kids from poor households may not have been able to consistently play sport.

ACKNOWLEDGEMENTS

To the two Bulldog scouts who offered me that first scholarship, which was signed on Mum's little Honda Civic all those years ago: Mark Hughes and John Ackland.

Over the course of my professional career, these people I'd humbly say are the unsung ones who hold some of these successful franchises together:

Peter and Mary Durose: although they could never replace Mum and Dad, this couple looked after me and many other young aspiring players living away from home at such a young age and did their best to be there and make it better.

Fred Ciraldo was at the Bulldogs for years and he took a shy young Islander boy under his wing and it meant the world to me.

Garry Carden was my first-ever professional trainer and his relentless training methods really laid the foundations for my steely attitude towards the physical and mental training demands required over my career and that I'm still using in the boxing ring to this day.

Cathy King from the Roosters. This lady, who most of us lads call 'Aunty', is a big part of the club's success. Thank you for always going above and beyond for me and my loved ones.

Keegan Smith and Patty Lane are two of the most knowledgeable trainers I've ever come across. Their personal help over the years has helped keep me at my physical best.

Victoria Hood, from the Auckland Blues. Thank you for helping a fourteen-year-old high school dropout achieve something he never thought possible – getting a Bachelor degree. You have given me the confidence to give it a go and I can now show my children what they can achieve in this world through education not just sports. Thanks, Vic!

All Blacks manager Darren Shand, thanks for your support over the years, brother.

The Chairman of the New Zealand Rugby Union, Brent Impey, and the rest of the board for their support on and off the field, especially for me and the Muslim community after the Christchurch attacks. Your support will always be remembered.

Chris Lendrum, your honest and forward-thinking approach made my contract dealings simple and straightforward. Thanks, bro.

To the Nasser brothers: Ammar, Khoder, Amin and Ahmed. Thank you for your loyalty, wisdom and brotherhood.

To my mum, dad, brother, sisters, nieces and nephews. Alhamdulillah, I've been blessed with you all in my life.

My wife, Alana, and children, Imaan, Aisha, Zaid and Essa.

Alana, I appreciate all you do for me and the kids and your love and support doesn't go unnoticed. I love you. Insha Allah, Allah continues to help us with the wisdom required to support our children to succeed in this world and the next.

Imaan, Aisha, Zaid and Essa (and God willing a few more to come), thank you for all the joy and challenges you bring to our lives. Without you all, our household wouldn't be the loud, loving place that it is. And without the blessings of your little souls, Alana and I wouldn't have the natural growth one has in raising four Mashallah children.

My life has been a journey of many mistakes, many selfish acts and misdemeanours towards myself and others. For all those I have offended or mistreated, I ask for your forgiveness. I thank the Most High for allowing me to learn from my mistakes and change my selfish ways. I pray that the Most Merciful continues to shine that mercy on me.

Index